The Crime Junkie's Guide
to Criminal Law

The Crime Junkie's Guide to Criminal Law

From *Law & Order* to Laci Peterson

Jim Silver

Westport, Connecticut
London

Library of Congress Cataloging-in-Publication Data

Silver, Jim, 1963–
    The crime junkie's guide to criminal law : from Law and order to Laci Peterson /
Jim Silver.
        p.   cm.
    Includes bibliographical references and index.
    ISBN: 978–0–275–99414–3 (alk. paper)
    1. Criminal law—United States—Popular works.   2. Criminal procedure—United
States—Popular works.   I. Title.
    KF9219.6.S55   2008
    345.73—dc22   2007036173

British Library Cataloguing in Publication Data is available.

Library of Congress Catalog Card Number: 2007036173
ISBN: 978–0–275–99414–3

First published in 2008

Praeger Publishers, 88 Post Road West, Westport, CT 06881
An imprint of Greenwood Publishing Group, Inc.
www.praeger.com

Printed in the United States of America

The paper used in this book complies with the
Permanent Paper Standard issued by the National
Information Standards Organization (Z39.48-1984).

10   9   8   7   6   5   4   3   2   1

For Julie

Contents

Contents

Preface

Let's face it, as long as it's not happening to you, crime is pretty entertaining. Every offense, from shoplifting to murder, combines danger and excitement with emotions like greed, anger, and the urge to make very close friends in prison. The dastardly deeds are often outrageous and sometimes hair-raising, but we can't seem to rip our eyes from the wreckage criminals make of their own lives and the lives of their victims. The dark side of human behavior both repulses and fascinates us.

Which is why stories about crime are all around us. From *Dragnet* to *Law & Order* and *CSI*, some of the most popular shows in television history have been and are about crime. Of course, it is not just fictional crime that interests us; we love to have actual cases brought into our living rooms courtesy of Court TV and documentary shows like A&E's *City Confidential* and *Cold Case Files*. News shows and magazines fairly drip with salacious details about the infamous evildoings of the moment.

However, unless you're a lawyer, you could probably use a little help making sense of the crime stories you see and read about every day. That's what this book is for—to give you a better understanding of criminal law. Maybe you know the *Miranda* warnings by heart, but do you know the difference between voluntary and involuntary manslaughter? Whether the police always need a warrant to search a private residence? What a fair trial really means? This book gives you the answers to those and many other questions. And, since there's no law against learning being fun,

The Crime Junkie's Guide illustrates key points with details from real-life trials and plots from your favorite shows.

While laws vary from state to state and no book could cover all the possible permutations, this book gives you the tools to evaluate relevant issues in real and fictional criminal cases. In other words, you will get the benefit of going to law school without the boring lectures. As an added bonus, you won't owe $100,000 in loans at the end of the book—although, feel free to send me that amount if you would like.

Acknowledgments

I was very fortunate to have the opportunity to write a book about the television shows that I love to watch. I would like to thank Richard Rosen for helping me develop the concept of "research via the remote"—there are few greater pleasures in life than settling into a couch and grabbing the TV remote control for a night of work. I also want to thank my wife and children for their support and encouragement. Finally, I am very grateful to my agent, Linda Konner, for her wonderful efforts on my behalf.

Chapter 1

Setting the Stage

Before getting to the juicy issues like murder and search warrants, it will be worthwhile to briefly step back for a broader view. It's always easier to see how the pieces fit together once you know the basic framework of the structure. And that's what criminal law is, a construction of rules based on tradition, reason, and practicality that helps define our social conduct and how far the government can go in regulating that conduct.

In this chapter we'll look at some of the basic principles of our system of criminal justice—how criminal law differs from other areas of the law, who is responsible for making criminal laws, etc. In the next chapter, we'll explore the common elements found in every crime and what they mean. Then we'll get right into knocking people off.

What Is Criminal Law?

A good starting point for thinking about criminal law is to realize that a crime is whatever the government says it is. Yes, that is circular reasoning and yes, there are many philosophical and historical musings that could be used to develop a more nuanced definition, but this does the job quite well. Keep in mind that not all bad behavior is criminal (being rude to a server) and some behavior many don't consider "bad" is criminalized (recreational drug use).

The object of criminal law is to punish bad behavior, and it is distinguished in two important ways from *civil law* (where people try to settle disagreements by private suits in court—your neighbor sues her contractor for shoddy repair work).

The first is that crime is a *public matter*. The state (meaning also the federal government) is responsible for protecting the public good, so actions that the state decides harm the public good are defined as crimes. When Mike Tyson was charged with rape in 1991, it was because his attack on an eighteen-year-old Miss Black America Pageant contestant named Desiree Washington in an Indianapolis hotel room was an attack on the public order.

The state of Indiana, like all states, seeks to protect its citizens from sexual assaults by having a statute on its books making these incidents criminal. The matter is thereby transformed from a situation where a young woman seeks to protect herself against a man who has wronged her, to one where the state seeks justice not only on her behalf but also on behalf of the public peace and tranquility.

The second and related way in which criminal law differs from civil law is that it involves an aspect of moral condemnation for bad behavior. When your neighbor sues her contractor, she is trying to recover money to compensate for damage done to her house and her peace of mind. A dispute over the installation of kitchen cabinets is not something that necessarily affects anyone else. A criminal act is a violation of a *communal* sense of decency. The state, on behalf of all its citizens, is charged not only with restoring order by removing wrongdoers from society (when appropriate) but also with expressing our shared outrage at the criminal's behavior. Criminal cases involve an element of punishment and condemnation that goes beyond attempting to compensate someone for economic loss and hurt feelings.

Since crime is a public concern, the state appears in court in the person of the public prosecutor, usually called a district attorney or a state's attorney. The district attorney (or state's attorney) is *not* working for the victim in the case. It is the state's case, and the victim is essentially another witness in the state's prosecution of the defendant for harm to the public welfare. Of course, the victim and his feelings will be considered by the state, but the victim doesn't get to call the shots. In fact, the victim doesn't even have to be a witness in the trial. Which stands to reason; it would be messy to keep a murder victim in court during a trial. In a 2006 episode of *CSI: Miami* called "Double Jeopardy" (#90), the DA prosecuted a husband for the murder of his wife even though the wife's body hadn't been found. As you recall, the DA still had to prove by inference that the wife was dead (she hadn't been seen in months, her credit card hadn't been used during that time, etc.).

The opposite situation sometimes occurs where the victim is alive and available for court, but does not want the defendant prosecuted. In a *Law & Order: SVU* episode entitled "Limitations" (#14), the squad is desperately trying to identify a serial rapist from DNA samples. Detectives Munch and Jeffries speak with one of the victims named Jennifer Neal, who tells them that although the rape was the worst thing that ever happened to her, the aftermath was the best thing. She was in a deep depression following the attack, but her friends pulled her out of it and gave her a new perspective on life.

As the investigation continues, Neal tells Detectives Benson and Stabler that she no longer wants to pursue the case. She lets slip that she actually knows who the rapist is and has spent time talking with him. She is a Quaker and fervently believes that the man has turned his life around and should not have to pay for what he did to her. The detectives are unwilling to abide by her wishes. They eventually have a judge lock her up when she refuses to identify her attacker (because she refused to obey a material witness order).

In most cases where a witness does not want to cooperate, the judicial system will commonly abide by her wishes (why put public resources into things like a spat over a fender-bender when the participants don't want any help?). Nevertheless, there are instances where the crime is so serious an offense against the public order (and maybe even other victims) that the judicial system will forge ahead and force cooperation from victims or proceed without any cooperation.

The Players

You should also keep in mind the different parts in the system. Recall the famous voice-over at the start of *Law & Order*: "In the criminal justice system, the people are represented by two separate yet equally important groups, the police who investigate the crimes and the district attorneys who prosecute the offenders. These are their stories." Although we may have a tendency to think of them as being one big, happy crime-fighting family, they really are separate organizations with differing priorities, budgets, operating systems, and hierarchies. Throw in the court system, which is separate from both the police and the district attorney, and you can imagine how the various players might frustrate one another.

The police might arrest someone on a felony offense, the district attorney's office could decide to charge it as a misdemeanor, and the judge might press the district attorney's office to drop the case entirely to relieve pressure on an overburdened trial schedule. Of course, there are the criminal defense lawyers who advocate for their clients and are also separate players in the system. If you want to think of this as a criminal justice "family," you'd better think of a dysfunctional one.

Where the Law Comes From

The original source of our criminal law was English law that was made by judges and was referred to as "common law." The colonies adopted this common law as their own criminal law. American courts then continued the tradition of deciding what behavior was criminal. That is no longer how things work in our country. Most states have formally abolished common law and replaced it with statutes passed by the legislature. Those that have not done away with common law have enacted statutes that largely supersede it.

While each state has the authority to create criminal laws that protect the public order in that state, the federal government also creates criminal law in certain circumstances. For example, the federal government makes criminal laws that govern the District of Columbia and national parks and territories. Federal criminal power also extends to aircraft and ships over and on the high seas. When a driver gets behind the wheel after a night of drinking, it's a state crime, and punishments vary from state to state. When a pilot who's been drinking gets into the cockpit of a commercial airliner, no matter where the airport, it's a federal crime carrying a penalty of up to fifteen years in jail. The federal government also makes laws that protect its agencies and employees.

While federal criminal law isn't involved in most cases (the vast majority of criminal cases are state matters), it can come into play in several ways. In episode #26 of *The Closer* an apparent attempt to kill a federally protected witness instead resulted in the murder of an FBI agent and the wife of the witness. Both the FBI and L.A.'s Priority Homicide Department show up at the murder scene and jockey for the right to run the investigation. FBI agent Hecht, who was responsible for protecting the witness, wants the FBI to run the show because a federal agent was killed. As is her way, Deputy Chief Brenda Johnson (with the support of Chief Pope) bluntly inserts herself and her department into the investigation on the basis that the murdered woman was neither a federal agent nor a federal witness. It doesn't hurt her position that the L.A. police actually take physical custody of the protected witness and question him. Eventually, the FBI and the police work out an arrangement to investigate the case jointly.

In real life, investigations and prosecutions sometimes involve both federal and state agencies and sometimes the agencies of more than one state. Where competing interests are at stake, decisions about who will investigate what and who will prosecute often come down to practical considerations.

An infamous multiple-jurisdiction case is the Beltway sniper attacks. Over a three-week period in 2002, John Allen Muhammed and Lee Boyd Malvo went on a shooting spree in and around Washington, D.C., the Baltimore-Washington metropolitan area, and Virginia. They killed ten people and critically injured three others in an apparent attempt to extort $10 million from the U.S. government.

Montgomery County (Maryland) Police Chief Charles Moose led the investigation with assistance from the FBI and D.C. and Virginia police. Although most of the shootings took place in Maryland, and both Maryland and Virginia had strong evidence against the men, the first trial was in Virginia (partly because Virginia allows the death penalty). After the two were convicted in Virginia, Virginia and Maryland prosecutors reached an agreement whereby Muhammed and Malvo were sent to Maryland for prosecution and then returned to Virginia.

LOCATION, LOCATION, LOCATION

Not only is it the most important rule in real estate, it is sometimes the determining factor in where a trial will be held. In a headline-making 2007 case from Kansas, Edwin R. Hall was charged with first-degree murder and aggravated kidnapping in the abduction and death of eighteen-year-old Kelsey Smith. Part of the evidence against Hall was a grainy security video from a Target store where Smith was last seen alive. The local district attorney said that it was unclear whether the case would be tried in federal or state court, noting that it is a federal offense to cross state lines while committing a kidnapping that results in death (Smith's body was discovered in Missouri). At the time of the arrest, the authorities were not clear on where Smith had been killed, but the district attorney said that the case would be tried in the jurisdiction that "provides the most severe penalty."

Substance vs. Procedure

Criminal law is broadly divided into *substantive law* and *procedural law*. *Substantive law* provides general principles of liability and defines particular crimes. For example, substantive criminal law tells us when someone is liable as a conspirator and tells us what exactly the state has to prove to convict him of that crime. *Procedural law* deals with the way in which crimes are investigated and guilt is determined. We're talking about things like search warrants, police interrogations, and juries. However, things get a little tricky with procedural law.

Both federal and state criminal laws have to comply with the U.S. Constitution. Obviously, the federal government is governed by the Constitution and the Bill of Rights, but the idea that states' criminal justice systems are also governed by the Constitution is relatively new. Starting roughly in the 1960s, the U.S. Supreme Court began relying on language in the Fourteenth Amendment to apply certain parts of the Bill of Rights to the states. This is known in legal circles as "selective incorporation."

In addition, states have their own constitutions, and the general principle is that while state constitutions cannot *limit* federal constitutional rights, they can *expand* them. A state constitution might provide a defendant more protection from searches and seizures than the Fourth Amendment provides. Suffice it to say then that state courts are still generally quite active in the area of *criminal procedure*.

One last general issue. Most states classify as felonies any crime punishable by death or imprisonment of a year or more. This includes all the serious crimes like murder, rape, burglary, robbery, mayhem, and other offenses that vary by state. Any crime that is punishable by less than a year in prison or by fine only is a misdemeanor. Note that it does not matter what the actual sentence is; it's what the punishment *could* be that defines the crime as a felony or misdemeanor. If someone is charged with felony robbery but for some particular reasons (first offense, sympathetic life story, lenient judge) is sentenced to only nine months in prison, the conviction is still a felony conviction since the possible punishment (stated in the applicable statute) is more than one year in prison.

Burden of Persuasion

As you undoubtedly know from all the hours you've logged watching *Cops*, all defendants are considered innocent until *proven* guilty. A fundamental tenet of our trial system is that the prosecution must prove that the defendant is guilty beyond a reasonable doubt of each and every element of the crime charged.

This means that the prosecution has to produce evidence that the defendant meets each element of the crime. This evidence could be in the form of eyewitness testimony, the results of scientific tests, a confession, circumstantial evidence, etc. Importantly, the defendant is *not* required to do anything to prove his innocence—not produce a single sliver of evidence to contradict the prosecution's case, not cross-examine the prosecution witnesses. A defendant and his lawyer could sit mute during a trial and the jury could return a "not guilty" verdict (of course, this is only theoretical—a lawyer could never remain silent for that long).

Beyond a Reasonable Doubt

You might think that such an important term as "reasonable doubt" has a standard definition that is set in stone. You'd be wrong. The Supreme Court has declined to adopt a set definition, and states use various formulations. It is clear, though, that "probable" guilt is not enough and that "absolute certainty" is not required.

In addition, the very high standard of "beyond a reasonable doubt" applies only to the defendant's guilt; other decisions made by the judge—whether evidence is admissible, whether a defendant's waiver of his rights was voluntary—can be made using a less strict standard, such as "by the preponderance of the evidence."

The burden of persuasion is not always the prosecution's, however; in cases where the defendant wishes to argue a defense that her actions were *excused* (for example, because of insanity) or *justified* (think self-defense), the defendant bears the burden of producing evidence to support the claim. These defenses (which go beyond merely contradicting or undermining the prosecution's case) are known as *affirmative defenses*.

If a defendant wishes to rely on an affirmative defense, she has to do more than talk about it in the opening statement—she must produce evidence to support it. Again, this could be in the form of witness testimony, test results, etc. Here the prosecution can if it so chooses sit back and see if the defendant can carry the burden. If the defendant cannot produce enough evidence to support the affirmative defense, the trial judge will generally not allow the jury to consider it in deliberations.

Of course, the prosecution is free to produce its own evidence to contradict the defendant's affirmative defense, but whether it in fact does may be decided by whether the defense has presented a believable affirmative defense in the first place.

Overall, the "burden of persuasion" issue is important because it has a lot to do with trial strategy. Generally speaking, it is easier to disprove than to prove, and it's usually better to have the other side show its cards first (as when they have the burden of persuasion) so you can know what you're dealing with and what you need to do to counter that evidence.

Legal Briefs

Common law—English judge-made law that was later adopted by individual states.

Substantive criminal law—The law usually contained in statute books that contains general principles of criminal liability and defines the elements of each particular criminal offense.

Procedural law—The law that deals with the ways in which crimes are investigated, guilt is determined, and punishment is given (how the police and courts function). Generally found in statute books, but also determined by courts.

Selective incorporation—The concept by which the U.S. Supreme Court has held that certain parts of the Bill of Rights also apply to the states.

State constitutions—Contain their own protections for the rights of citizens; may not limit federal constitutional rights, but may expand them.

Felony—Any crime punishable by a year or more in prison.

Misdemeanor—Any crime punishable by less than a year in prison or a fine only.

Chapter 2

Recipe for Crime

It's shortly after Christmas, 2002, and you pick your newspaper up off the front stoop. Looking below the fold, you notice a story about a young, pregnant woman who has gone missing in California. The woman, eight months pregnant with her first child, was last seen on the morning of Christmas Eve, when her husband left their house to go on a fishing trip some eighty miles away. The husband says that his wife's plans were to take their dog for a walk in the park and then go grocery shopping. He says that she was not at home when he returned from his trip. He reported her missing that night, and a $500,000 reward was posted for information leading to the return of the mother-to-be.

Within a week of the woman's disappearance, the story is being followed by every major news organization in the country. You can't turn on the television or pick up a paper without seeing a picture of the young mother. The police are convinced that they are dealing with foul play. By mid-January the volunteer search center has closed. On January 30, a woman admits to having had an affair with the husband and acknowledges that she has been working with the police, even tape-recording conversations with the husband.

In mid-April, after the bodies of the wife and unborn infant boy wash ashore in the San Francisco Bay, Scott Peterson is arrested for the murder of Laci Peterson and Connor Peterson, and one of the most celebrated and heavily covered criminal trials in American history is set to begin. The trial started in June 2004, and in November 2004, Peterson was convicted of killing both Laci and Connor.

Unbelievably, this heinous crime of murdering a young mother and her unborn baby shares certain characteristics with every other crime committed in America, from a pickpocket snatching the wallet of an un-suspecting tourist to the Lindbergh baby kidnapping. These two fundamental elements of every crime are a *physical act* done with a particular *state of mind*.

VICTIMS

According to the *Criminal Victimization in the United States, 2005 Statistical Tables*, in 2005, U.S. residents age twelve and older experienced approximately 23 million crimes. Of these, 77 percent were property crimes, and 23 percent were crimes of violence (Table 1).

Physical Act

American criminal law punishes only acts and in some cases failure to act; it does not punish mere thoughts—undoubtedly a good thing for every employee who has ever thought about swiping a little from the till and every neighbor who has wanted to slug the guy running his leaf-blower at dawn. For all the times you've heard the phrase "thought police" thrown around in political discourse, the real thing doesn't exist. Obviously, we can't read people's minds. If we could, we'd still have the problem of distinguishing between thoughts that would lead to societal harm (and should be punishable) and thoughts that are harmless, fleeting notions.

Even though there was evidence that Scott Peterson told his mistress, Amber Frey, that Laci had died the year before she actually went missing, he was not charged with *wishing* that Laci were dead or *pretending* that she was dead; he was charged with actually doing something to end Laci and Connor's lives.

CRIMINAL SPEECH

It's important to understand that "speech" is not "thought" for purposes of criminal law. While you can't be prosecuted for something you think, you can be prosecuted for something you've *said*. For certain crimes (solicitation, perjury), speech is the act that is criminalized.

The basic criminal law definition is that an act is some *"bodily movement made voluntarily."* It's helpful to consider separately the two parts of this definition. The bodily movement part is pretty straightforward—it means things like lighting the match to the gasoline-soaked rags in the basement, pulling the trigger.

STATUS CRIMES

The Supreme Court has held that making a crime out of a "status" instead of a physical act is unconstitutional: A state cannot make it a crime to be an "addict" or an "alcoholic." The reasoning is that just because someone has a particular character trait does not necessarily mean that she will somehow disrupt the public order. On the other hand, states are free to define *acts* such as public drunkenness as crimes, even though the act is directly related to the person's status.

Some crimes state specifically the act the defendant must have committed (burglary requires "breaking and entering"), but homicide statutes are different. They don't designate the exact act the defendant must have done that results in the killing. Thus, pretty much any physical movement that causes an unlawful taking of life can be a homicide. Interestingly, in the *Peterson* case, the prosecution was unable to pinpoint the cause of Laci's death (the body was badly decomposed by the time it was recovered). The theory the prosecution presented to the jury was that Scott either strangled or smothered Laci before dumping her body. The jury believed one of the two.

The "voluntary" part of the act means that the bodily movement must be a conscious and willful one. Acts done while the person is unconscious or even asleep are usually not criminal. (Being unconscious or asleep is not the same thing as having an *altered* state of consciousness, as with mental illness or some type of intoxication. The law controlling claims of insanity and intoxication is covered in later chapters.)

You may recall the 1997 case of an Arizona man, Scott Falater, that received quite a bit of media attention including a special program on Court TV. Falater stabbed his wife forty-four times with a hunting knife, dragged her outside where he held her head underwater in their pool, hid the knife, and went to bed. A neighbor saw the attack by the pool and called the police. The police arrived to find Falater with bandages on his hands and blood on his neck.

Falater claimed to have no knowledge of the vicious murder and claims that he must have been sleepwalking at the time. His long history of sleepwalking was confirmed by friends and family, and he argued at trial that he was not criminally responsible because he had not acted consciously.

The jury did not believe his story and found him guilty of first-degree murder.

KNOWLEDGE OF PENDING UNCONSCIOUSNESS

A person may be found criminally responsible for acts committed while unconscious if she knew that she might become unconscious and cause some harm. Thus, even if the jury had believed that Falater was sleepwalking when he killed his wife, they might properly have found him guilty if he had a history of violence during his sleepwalking episodes.

Sometimes it's not what you do; it's what you didn't do that lands you in trouble. Although this seems counterintuitive because we've been talking about acts, in certain circumstances a person may be found criminally liable for doing nothing (failing to act). All those times when you were a kid and you were punished by your parents despite protesting "I didn't do anything!" may not have been unfair after all. A person can be found guilty of failing to act where:

1. The person was under a duty to act;
2. The person had the necessary knowledge;
3. The person was physically capable of acting.

A "duty to act" is commonly found where there is a special relationship, like mother to child or husband to wife. The duty could also be created by a contract (a caretaker for an elderly person) or even by a voluntary assumption of care, like where relative agrees to care for a child.

Mental State

The second piece of every crime is the "mental element." To be considered a crime, a person must do some physical act (or, in some cases, not do some physical act) *with a particular state of mind*. The principle is that society should only punish those who have a "guilty mind" because they are more blameworthy than those who accidentally do wrong. Some would also argue that society gets more bang for its law enforcement buck by focusing on those who knowingly offend, i.e., the most dangerous and likely to reoffend (how can we discourage those who never intended to cause any harm?) This "mental element" is often a crucial area of dispute in a trial.

Even if the prosecution can prove that the defendant did a certain act, the defendant can't be convicted unless there is also proof that she had the requisite state of mind while doing that act.

Although there are an infinite number of attitudes and motivations that a person can feel in a day, criminal law focuses on a few mental states. The traditional criminal states of mind are *general intent, specific intent,* and *criminal negligence. General intent* simply means the intent to commit the act that constitutes the crime. This is the "default" mental state for any crime that requires more than criminal negligence but which does not require specific intent. General intent does not need to be expressly shown, but can be inferred from the doing of the act; in other words, we presume that people intend the acts that they voluntarily do. Some statutes may use words such as "willfully" or "deliberately," which mean the same thing as general intent.

In *specific intent* crimes, the statute will require not only the doing of an act, but also the doing of it with a specific intent. Specific intent crimes are "general intent crimes *plus* another intent." Unlike with general intent, this other specific intent cannot be inferred and must be proven. Specific intent crimes are things like burglary (must show intent to commit a felony in the dwelling), solicitation (must show intent to have the person commit the crime), and robbery (must show intent to permanently deprive victim of property).

MOTIVE

This may be splitting hairs, but motive is *not* the same thing as intent. Motive is the reason a crime was committed (the defendant hated the victim; the defendant needed money to feed a gambling addiction). For all the talk you hear from TV cops and DAs about "establishing the motive" for a crime, the only thing the prosecution legally has to show is that the defendant did the prohibited act with the intent required by the statute. While a showing of motive may be a reliable indicator that the defendant committed the crime, the law does not require the prosecution to show any motive at all on the defendant's part in order to prove guilt beyond a reasonable doubt. Whether the jury will convict without having a story as to why the crime occurred is an entirely separate question.

With some crimes, like involuntary manslaughter, liability can be based on *criminal negligence,* which means that the defendant acted with a "gross" lack of care. This is a higher standard than ordinary negligence in the civil law context. To find that an act rises to the level of a crime, the prosecution must show more than that the defendant failed to exercise due care; the defendant's action must have involved a high degree of unreasonableness.

There are actually some crimes that don't have any mental state requirement at all. These are referred to as *strict liability* offenses and generally mean that there is no state of mind with regard to certain factors constituting the crime. They are usually part of some government regulatory scheme, although the one people are most familiar with is statutory rape.

A final consideration for "mental state" requirements is something called "transferred intent." This is what is known in the law profession as a "legal fiction" (insert your own joke here) and it comes into play in situations where the defendant doesn't accomplish exactly what he set out to do but nevertheless causes harm. Here's a typical transferred intent scenario, courtesy of a 2007 episode of *Law & Order* (#384):

A near riot breaks out at Grammercy University when controversial conservative political pundit Judith Barlow speaks to a group of students. The give-and-take between Barlow and students in the audience becomes increasingly volatile until some of the students try to rush the stage. In the melee, a gunshot rings out and student Jason Miles falls dead, shot through the heart by Malcolm Yates, a graduate student at Grammercy.

Here's the twist—Yates is a scientific researcher with Parkinson's disease and Barlow happens to be a prominent critic of stem-cell research, which may hold promise in finding a cure for Parkinsons. Yates did in fact fire the gun, but he intended to kill Barlow that evening, not his friend and fellow protester Jason Miles. Therein the conundrum: If Yates did not *intend* to shoot Miles at all, is Yates guilty of murder? In our criminal justice system, the answer is "yes." The law rationalize that the defendant's mental state with regard to his intended victim "transfers" to the actual victim. As Jack McCoy puts it to Yates during a plea bargaining session in the standard *Law & Order* conference room sequence—"I'm sure your lawyer can explain to you, Mr. Yates, that in criminal law, intent follows the bullet."

The Model Penal Code Approach to Mental States

In the 1950s, a group of law professors, judges, and lawyers proposed a model penal code as a guide for legislatures. Although the proposal, referred to as the MPC, has no legal authority, some states have simply adopted parts of the MPC and others have modified MPC provisions to fit their statutory schemes. An important facet of the MPC (and now many state codes) is that it replaces traditional principles such as general and specific intent with four definitions of mental states—*purposely, knowingly, recklessly,* and *negligently.*

According to the MPC, a person acts *purposely* where she has a conscious desire to act in a certain way or to cause a certain outcome. A person acts *knowingly* where she is practically certain that her conduct will cause a particular result. *Recklessly* means that the person is aware of a substantial risk that his conduct will cause the result. Unlike with *knowingly,* where the defendant must be certain of the outcome, *recklessly* means the prosecution only has to show that the defendant *was aware* of a considerable risk to others. A person acts *negligently* where he *should have been aware* of a substantial risk; in other words, where a reasonable person would have been aware of the risk. The major difference between *recklessly* and *negligently* is that *recklessly* requires a conscious awareness of the risk involved. Clear as mud, right? Let's take a real-life crime and play with it a little to illustrate these definitions.

In the early morning of September 15, 1963, Ku Klux Klan members Bobby Frank Cherry and Robert Edward Chambliss planted nineteen sticks of dynamite in the basement of the Sixteenth Street Baptist Church in Birmingham, Alabama. The church had been a rallying point for many civil rights activities and was an important symbol of the civil rights movement. Later that morning, approximately eighty children walked into the church basement for prayers and the bomb exploded, killing four young girls—Addie Mae Collins, Carole Robertson, Cynthia Wesley, and Denise McNair—and injuring almost two dozen others.

Assume that the bombers' objective was to destroy the church and kill church members; obviously, they acted *purposely* to bring about this desired result by planting the dynamite in the church basement on a Sunday morning. Next, assume a slightly different scenario where the bombers' objective was solely to destroy the building but that they also knew that the church basement would be occupied in the morning and that setting the bomb to go off at that time would kill some church members. The bombers still acted purposely with regard to destroying the church, but since they did not consciously desire the death of the church members, the bombers acted *knowingly* with regard to that tragic result.

Now, let's change the scenario again to one where the bombers' objective is still to destroy the church building, but that they plant the bomb to go off on a Tuesday evening, and that although they know that the church basement is used regularly during the week, they do not know exactly when the basement is used on Tuesdays. Suppose that in fact children and adults are in the basement engaged in religious education and are killed in the blast. The bombers would have acted *recklessly* with regard to these deaths since they were aware of a substantial risk that their conduct would result in some deaths.

Finally, suppose that the bombers set the bomb to go off in the early morning hours, believing that no one would be in the church at all, but that people are still killed. Assume also that the church was such an active establishment that any reasonable person would have been aware that the church might be in use at any hour of the day or night. The bombers would have acted *negligently* with regard to the people killed in the early morning blast.

REPORTING TO THE POLICE

According to the *Criminal Victimization in the United States, 2005 Tables*, during 2005 less than half of all violent crimes were reported to the police, and only 39 percent of all property crimes were reported. Interestingly, motor vehicle theft was reported to the police in nearly eight out of ten cases, while rape and sexual assault were reported barely over a third of the time (Table 91).

Legal Briefs

Elements of a crime—The physical act and mental state of the defendant that must be proven to convict.

General intent—The intent to commit the act that constitutes the crime; can be inferred from just the doing of the act.

Specific intent—The intent to do the act that constitutes the crime *plus* another particular purpose to the act (for larceny, must show intent to physically take the property *plus* the intent to permanently deprive the owner of the property). Cannot be inferred, must be proven.

Criminal negligence—A gross lack of care; a higher standard than civil negligence.

Transferred intent—A creative concept whereby courts rationalize that a defendant's mental state toward her intended victim is "transferred" to the actual victim.

Model Penal Code—A model penal code created in the 1950s by a group of law professors, judges, and lawyers. The MPC recognized four mental states:

Purposely—Where the defendant has the conscious desire to act in a certain way or cause a certain outcome.

Knowingly—Where the defendant is practically certain that a conduct will cause a particular result.

Recklessly—Where the defendant is aware of a substantial risk arising from the conduct.

Negligently—Where the defendant should have been aware of a substantial risk arising from the conduct.

Chapter 3

Homicide

Shakespeare and Dostoyevsky wrote a lot about homicide and not so much about tax evasion because, let's face it, knocking someone off is just good drama. Doing away with a human being involves tension, danger, brutality, and loads of emotion. It's not surprising that killing has long been a staple of our television entertainment—from *Kojak* to Court TV.

In fact, you've probably viewed more fictitious homicides than you realize. According to research done at the University of Nebraska, by the time most people reach the age of eighteen, they will have witnessed on television (with average viewing time) approximately *40,000* homicides. This is obviously a shocking figure since you will never experience this level of violence in your own life—unless, of course, you work the return counter at Macy's after the holidays.

Besides being dramatically interesting, homicide is obviously a serious crime and one that illustrates an important concept: criminal law is mostly about definitions. It doesn't really matter whether something seems "wrong," immoral, or unethical. If you can't point to the actual wording of a criminal statute or court decision that says it's a crime, it's not a crime. This makes sense. The whole purpose of substantive (as opposed to procedural) criminal law is to define what kinds of things will get you into hot water.

The definition of homicide is the killing of a human being by another human being. It comes from the Latin *homo* meaning "man" and *cide* meaning, "fleeing in a white Ford Bronco." Traditionally, homicides are subdivided into justifiable, excusable, and criminal homicides. While at first it may seem that any killing should merit years breaking rocks in the hot sun, common sense tells us that there is a world of difference between a woman snuffing her husband for the insurance money and a woman using deadly force to protect herself from an unprovoked street attack. The law also sees this distinction. The first two types of homicides—justifiable homicides and excusable homicides—are not punishable by criminal law.

A *justifiable* homicide is an intentional killing that is authorized by law because it is seen as socially acceptable. Like when some nitwit takes a cell phone call at the movie theater and starts barking orders to his, apparently, deaf assistant, and you . . . okay, that's not really one of them. What it *does* include is the execution of criminals in states with the death penalty, killing in self-defense, or killing to prevent a felony or capture a dangerous felon.

Consider the Amadou Diallo case, which was covered extensively by Court TV and the rest of the national media. On February 4, 1999, four plainclothes officers were patrolling in the Bronx, New York, when they saw Diallo standing inside a building vestibule and acting in a way they considered suspicious. Apparently thinking that Diallo was about to commit a robbery, the officers approached him and a series of fatal misperceptions followed.

According to the officers, Diallo ignored their commands to halt and "darted" to the back of the vestibule, where he reached into his pocket. The officers believed that Diallo was reaching for a gun. When one of the officers fell off the steps, his colleagues thought he had been shot and they opened fire. Amadou Diallo was hit nineteen times. In fact, Diallo was unarmed and carried only a beeper, a wallet, and his keys. The officers were charged with second-degree murder (and other lesser offenses as well). At trial, the defense scored a major victory when the judge agreed to instruct the jurors that they could acquit the officers if they believed that the officers had to use force to apprehend a fleeing felon. The jurors acquitted the officers on all charges.

An *excusable* homicide is one where the killer is not seen as morally culpable for the killing because the death is the result of an accident that occurred during a lawful act where people were using ordinary care in their actions. Doing something lawful with no care (burning some brush during a windstorm) and doing something illegal but with great care (pouring paint thinner in your rival's coffee without spilling a drop) will not qualify.

The idea behind excusable homicides is that the person who caused the death isn't at fault. Think of a sportsman following all the safety rules at a shooting range when suddenly, on a dare, some knucklehead runs across the line of fire and is killed. Unlike with a justifiable homicide, society doesn't exactly see the killing of knuckleheads as acceptable (or it would be open season on reality show contestants), but you probably don't think the sportsman should go to prison, and neither does the law.

Of course, most of the interesting homicides are the last type of homicide—good, old-fashioned criminal homicides: the ones where the police arrest the "perp" and sweat him in "the box" before he "lawyers-up." Criminal homicide abides no justifications or excuses. This is the world of "bumping off" and "rubbing out," of barbarous rages and fatal consequences. People who fit into this blameworthy category don't get a free pass; they get a prison ID number and worse. That is, if the police "collar up."

Truth will Come to Sight; Murder Cannot be Hid Long.
William Shakespeare, *The Merchant of Venice*

That's sure how it seems on TV; the cops and DAs get to the truth in murder cases with great regularity. Although the authorities sometimes stumble on *Law & Order*, in most shows an arrest is made in every murder case and trials end with guilty verdicts. Then there's the real world. According to the FBI's *Crime in the United States, 2005*, only 61 percent of all murders reported to the police were cleared by an arrest or other means. Thankfully, there are always cold-case squads like those depicted on A&E's *Cold Case Files* and CBS's *Cold Case*.

Criminal homicides themselves are generally divided into three different offenses: murder, which is a killing with malice aforethought; voluntary manslaughter, which is a killing after adequate provocation; and involuntary manslaughter, which is a negligent killing.

Legal Briefs

Homicide—A killing of one human being by another human being.

Justifiable homicide—A killing that is authorized by law (think of a police officer shooting an armed bank robber).

Excusable homicide—An accidental death where the killer deserves no punishment.

Chapter 4

⚖️

Murder

Imagine that you are the proud father of a high school hockey star. You sacrifice an enormous amount of time and money to help your son hone his skills because this sport is his ticket to college, something you otherwise might not be able to give him. For years you faithfully attend all his games and practices, cheering him on, urging him to skate even harder, score even more. Sometimes you get too involved, screaming at the coaches and referees, clashing with the parents of other players, even those on your son's team. But all you want is what's best for your boy. It's not your fault if other kids aren't as talented and if their parents can't handle that fact. The scouts need to see that your son is the best.

Now, imagine that one day the coach kicks your son out of practice and benches him for the next game because of a little rough play. When you hear the news, you are as angry as you've ever been. There are going to be college scouts at that game; this is what you and your son have been working toward since he was four. How could this idiot coach throw that away?

You confront the coach in the parking garage after practice, your son by your side. You want to know what the hell is going on and your fury only builds as you realize the coach isn't going to change his mind. In a blind rage, you punch the coach in the face, grab your son's stick, and whack the bastard good. Even that's not enough. Your son is yelling something at you, but you don't hear. You just see the cause of your trouble lying on the ground, blood streaming from his wounds, and you kick him. You'll kick that damn benching right out of him. Then you see that he's not moving anymore and a frightening thought breaks through your rage: you've gone too far. He's dead and you're the defendant in a *Law & Order* episode.

After the police figure out that it was your son who made the 911 call, they get a warrant and search your apartment, finding a hockey stick with blood on it. McCoy puts pressure on you and your son, even threatening to charge your boy, until you and your son agree he should testify against you—in your murder trial. It may seem obvious, but let's look at the reasons behind the charge. Why, as a matter of law, did your actions add up to murder?

Most states define murder as the unlawful killing of another human being with "malice aforethought." Remember, if it's a lawful killing, it's a justifiable homicide and not murder. Since none of the fifty states has legalized beating someone to death over a hockey game, this cannot be justifiable homicide.

It is important to know what "malice aforethought" means. One thing it means is that lawyers like to make things confusing by using lots of words that no one uses in their everyday lives, like "party of the first part," "heretofore," and "$500 an hour." Oddly, "malice aforethought" does *not* mean that the killer acted out of ill will or hatred toward the victim.

What "malice aforethought" does mean is that the defendant acted with at least one of the following mental states: (1) intent to kill, or (2) intent to inflict great bodily harm, or (3) extreme recklessness (in some states it's called "depraved indifference") as to whether the victim lived, or (4) intent to commit a felony during the commission (or attempted commission) of which someone dies. The key concept is that if a person kills someone and meets *any one* of these criteria, he is guilty of murder.

BY THE NUMBERS

The FBI's *Crime in the United States, 2005,* shows that there were almost 17,000 murders in 2005; of those, 63 percent were committed with a firearm, and 12.9 percent with a knife or cutting instrument.

Intent to Kill

An intentional killing means that the defendant actually *meant* to kill the victim. Trying to determine what the defendant was actually thinking poses a small difficulty in that there are no magical machines that can read someone's thoughts. To deal with that problem, the law generally assumes that ordinary people intend the natural and foreseeable consequences of their actions and allows the jury to infer the intent behind those actions.

In 1989, Lyle and Erik Menendez, each carrying a shotgun, burst into their family home where their parents, Jose and Kitty, were seated on a couch. The brothers fired their weapons, hitting Jose four times and Kitty nine times. Jose and Kitty were shot in the head and the extremities, and most of the shots to Kitty occurred when she was lying on the floor. Leaving aside allegations of cruelty and abuse that may have driven the brothers to such extremes (and which surely didn't hurt Court TV's ratings), it is clear that Lyle and Erik wanted their parents dead. There's no other way to view shooting someone multiple times with a shotgun. In fact, some states have what is referred to as the "deadly weapon rule." When a person intentionally uses a deadly weapon (such as a shotgun) against a vital part of the body (such as the head), the inference of intent to kill is assumed.

Back to our hockey dad. Did he intend to kill the coach? He surely meant to hurt him, as demonstrated by the punch to the face and the kick when the coach was on the ground. Those actions, by themselves, probably point to a man driven by anger to hurt, not necessarily kill. We don't usually think of a punch and a kick as leading to death.

But what about the hockey stick? Is it a deadly weapon (usually defined as anything designed to inflict death or serious physical injury)? Perhaps the prosecution could argue it is, but players swing hockey sticks at each other all the time in games, receiving nothing more than a penalty if they're caught doing it in a way prohibited by the rules. Even though the dad meant to hit the coach with the stick, it may not enough to meet the "intent to kill" standard.

Intent to Inflict Great Bodily Harm

Where a person causes serious bodily injury to a victim who then dies, malice aforethought is *implied*. The injury has to be something more than a superficial wound; it must be something that leads to a loss of consciousness, broken bones, or lots of suturing. Say you are arguing with your neighbor over her dog's barking and you shove her down on her plush lawn and, somehow, she dies. This is *not* "intent to inflict great bodily harm murder." But suppose you are having that same argument on her second-story deck and you push her off it and she dies—that's another story altogether. Anyone who intends to cause substantial injuries that ultimately result in death is guilty of murder. Although we don't know the exact extent of the injuries to the coach, he no doubt suffered serious bodily injury, and the hockey dad could have been charged with murder on this basis.

"YEAR AND A DAY RULE"

Most states used to have a rule that the defendant couldn't be prosecuted for murder unless the victim died within a year and a day of the attack. In other words, if the victim died a year and *two* days after the attack, the defendant could not be tried for murder (although she could still be charged with other crimes such as aggravated assault, etc.). The "year and a day" itself was an arbitrary period, but the purpose behind the rule was to try to guarantee that the victim died as a result of the attack itself and not from some unrelated (perhaps even natural) cause after a long period of time. With the advent of more modern medical and scientific techniques, we can much more accurately determine the cause of death without regard to the passage of time, and most states have done away with the rule.

Extreme Recklessness ("Depraved Heart")

Malice aforethought is again implied where the defendant shows an extreme indifference to the value of human life. Extreme recklessness, or as it is sometimes termed "depraved heart" murder, typically involves something like firing a gun at a building knowing that there may be people inside, or even failing to control dogs that have consistently shown very aggressive behavior.

The idea is that a defendant who may not have intended to kill should have known that his actions created an extremely high risk of a victim's demise. In our *Law & Order* episode, this is exactly the basis the DA used to prosecute the hockey dad. Violently attacking a man and then fleeing the scene shows that the father was more concerned with being caught than with whether the coach lived or died. At least the jury thought so, and they convicted the dad of second-degree murder.

Felony Murder Rule

Three women carrying shopping bags and dressed as Holly Golightly from *Breakfast at Tiffany's* enter Fieldcrest Jewelers in New York City. Once inside, they all pull sawed-off shotguns from their shopping bags and announce that they are robbing the store. They force the customers and employees, including the security guard, onto the floor, shatter the glass display cases, and begin grabbing the loot.

Suddenly the security guard rises and tries to tackle one of the robbers. She drops her shotgun and it slides across the floor. At that moment the store manager reaches underneath a table and activates a hidden alarm system. Security doors immediately drop to close off the exits. Unfortunately, for the store manager, one of the doors drops directly onto the shotgun that had been dropped onto the floor. The shotgun discharges, killing the store manager, who happened to be lying directly in its line of fire.

Surely the purpose of the robbery was not to kill the store manager. In fact, the bizarre set of circumstances leading to his death could hardly have been imagined by anyone. (Except, of course, for the writers of *CSI: NY*, who wrote this script for episode #49.) However, as CSI Lindsay Monroe noted in the show, the death occurred during a felony, bringing it under the felony murder rule and making the Hollys all responsible for the murder of the store manager.

In most states, a death that occurs during the commission or attempted commission of a specified dangerous felony (usually rape, robbery, burglary, and arson) is first-degree murder. If the death occurs during any other felony, the charge is second-degree murder. It doesn't matter whether the defendant intends to kill or it happens accidentally or even unforeseeably; if someone dies during the felony, the charge is murder. Therefore, whether a robber intentionally shoots the victim through the heart to do away with a witness or the victim dies of a heart attack while handing over her jewelry, or a door accidentally causes a shotgun to fire, the charge is still murder.

The main justification for such a strict rule is that it is meant to be a deterrent to those who might commit serious crimes. Perhaps they will reconsider or, if not, at least proceed with greater caution so as not to cause a death. Because, really, who is more likely to carefully consider the implications of his actions than a sweating, retching, strung-out addict who is desperate for money?

Of course, prosecutors love the felony murder rule because all they have to prove is that the defendant committed or attempted to commit the felony and that a death resulted; they don't have to prove any premeditation or malice aforethought.

An important consideration for applying this rule is what exactly constitutes "during the commission or attempted commission of a felony"? What are the beginning and end points of the felony? Courts commonly hold that the death must occur during the *res gestae* (things done) of the felony. This means that the rule applies from the instant the defendant has done enough to be charged with *attempting* the felony to the completion of the felony. Most courts agree that the felony continues, even after the commission of the crime, until the felon reaches a place of temporary safety. If an officer dies in an accident during a high-speed chase of a fleeing rapist, the felony murder rule would apply. If the officer has a heart attack the next day while searching for the rapist, the rule would not apply.

Not only must the death occur during the *res gestae* of the felony, the death must occur *because of* that felony. If a defendant is passing a bad check (a felony) and the clerk, who is unaware of the crime, dies of a heart attack during what he thinks is a normal transaction, the felony murder rule would not apply. Because of the potential harshness of the felony murder rule, some states also limit the rule to felonies that are inherently dangerous (rape, robbery, burglary, and arson). In those states, even if the clerk becomes aware that the defendant is passing a bad check and has a heart attack, the charge would *not* be murder.

Another important limitation put on the felony murder rule is significant for our *Law & Order* hockey dad. In some states, the rule only applies if the felony is *independent* of the death. If the felony is *not* independent, it is said to *merge* with the homicide. What this means is that if death occurs during an armed robbery, the felony murder rule applies since the purpose of the robbery—taking property—is independent of the death. However, in the case of a felonious assault, as with our hockey dad, the assaultive conduct that caused the death *is* the felony, and the felony murder rule does not apply. This makes sense. If there were no merger limitation, every voluntary and involuntary manslaughter would be bootstrapped into a felony murder and the entire purpose of having separate murder and manslaughter offenses would be defeated. Anyway, this is why McCoy had to use the "extreme indifference" theory to prosecute the hockey dad and couldn't rely on the easier-to-prove felony murder rule.

Killing by a Nonfelon

An interesting question arises when a death is caused by the *victim* of the crime shooting at the felon (think of a store clerk with a gun under the counter). What if the clerk/victim misses the felon and accidentally kills an innocent bystander? Can the felon be charged with felony murder for a death that resulted *not in furtherance* of the crime but *in resistance* to it? Probably not. However, some states *would* charge felony murder because the felon set in motion a chain of events that she should have realized might result in a death. In the store clerk example, it seems reasonable to hold the robber responsible for the foreseeable resistance to her initial armed assault. The application of the rule makes less sense where the felon shoplifts an expensive watch and the clerk opens fire. Presumably the shoplifter would not be prosecuted for felony murder if a death results.

GETTING IT (MOSTLY) RIGHT

An abstract, published in 2003, in *The Journal of Criminal Justice and Popular Culture* entitled "Prime Time Murder: Presentation of Murder on Popular Justice Programs" found that the murders presented on *Law & Order* are consistent with the patterns shown by official statistics. Murder is male-perpetrated (approximately 88 percent), usually committed by an individual known to the victim (1976–2002, almost 52 percent of murderers were known to the victim, 13.9 percent were strangers and the remainder were undetermined), and often occurring in conjunction with a felony (1976–2002, 79 percent of male victims, and 22 percent of female victims were killed during the commission of a felony). This show (and others) also correctly depicts murder as a predominantly intraracial act that often takes place in the victim's home or on the street. However, television dramas tend to underemphasize knives as murder weapons (approximately 13 percent of homicides in 2002) and give the incorrect impression that most murders are planned when, in fact, they're not.

Degree of Murder

Many state statutes divide murder into first and second-degree, with only first-degree murderers eligible for the death penalty. Generally speaking, killing by means of lying in wait, poison, bomb, torture, or during the course of certain violent felonies (such as arson, burglary, rape, and robbery) is first-degree murder. In addition, most states provide that "willful, deliberate, and premeditated" murders are first-degree. All other murders are second-degree.

While this may seem straightforward, a consistent difficulty with distinguishing first-degree from second-degree murder has been defining the limits of "deliberate and premeditated" (most courts agree that "willful" simply means "intentional"). Some courts see "deliberate" as meaning "consider" or "evaluate." They hold that the killer must have actually reflected on the idea of killing, weighing the consequences of the act. Someone who kills because of excitement or a "sudden passion" has not deliberated and is not guilty of first-degree murder. Other courts, however, see "deliberate" as nearly synonymous with "willful" and treat nearly all intentional homicides as first-degree.

The concept of "premeditated" has also been problematic. The dictionary definition of premeditated is "consciously considered beforehand." The tricky question is *how much* time beforehand? Some courts have held that a defendant's reflection and ultimate decision to kill can occur as quickly as successive thoughts. In other words, they are not talking about days or even hours; seconds will suffice. Another view is that it takes *some* greater length of time for a person to consider murder, and factors such as degree of planning and manner of killing should be considered in the evaluation.

Then there is the question of what evidence is sufficient to demonstrate premeditation. Some courts uphold verdicts of premeditated murder where the evidence shows that the defendant had *enough time* for an opportunity to premeditate and the jury found that he in fact did. Other courts require *direct proof* that the defendant made the decision to kill after calm deliberation.

In episode #143 of *CSI*, Grissom and Sara investigate the murder of an aging rock star in his kitchen and discover nearby an exact half-inch-scale replica of the crime scene, complete with some of the victim's actual blood in the model, pooled in the same pattern as the victim's. As Sara notes, the model shows a level of obsession to detail that must have taken weeks if not months to prepare. Obviously whoever murdered rock star Izzy must have been thinking about it for a long time and would have a tough time arguing that the killing was not premeditated. Things are rarely that clear in the real world.

So difficult is it for courts to distinguish between degrees of murder that some states have done away with the distinction entirely and instead rely on a set of aggravating and mitigating criteria for establishing the severity of the punishment. These criteria usually address both the nature of the murder (was it especially cruel, for example) as well as the defendant himself (his criminal history).

In a 2007 case that made national headlines, a thirty-three-year-old mother of four was found guilty of first-degree murder for killing her Marine husband in order to collect on $250,000 in veteran's pay. The jury found Cynthia Sommer guilty of "special allegations" of administering poison (her husband Todd was found to have more than one thousand times the normal level of arsenic in his liver) and killing for financial gain (soon after collecting the money Cynthia had breast implant surgery and began hosting loud parties at their home). After her conviction of first-degree murder with special allegations, Cynthia was given a mandatory sentence of life in prison without parole.

A fictional example of "special circumstances" was in episode #9 of *Shark* called "Dial M for Monica." In that show a deputy DA is gunned down along with a high-priced hooker. It turns out that this particular hooker was starting her own escort business, and the woman for whom she worked was so upset that she paid a drug dealer $75,000 to kill the hooker (the deputy DA just happened to be there because he was trying to get information from the hooker to build a case against a major drug lord). As Sebastian *Stark* tells the jury in his opening statement, some types of "special circumstance murders" are so evil that they can bring the death penalty—and murder-for-hire is one of those circumstances.

Looking again at our *Law & Order* hockey dad, you can understand why he was convicted of second-degree murder. He didn't use poison, a bomb, or torture to kill, and he didn't beat the coach to death during one of the typically enumerated violent felonies like robbery or burglary. It's also pretty clear that he didn't "evaluate" or "consider beforehand" his actions; he got into an argument and lost control of his emotions—classic second-degree murder in most states, and on *Law & Order*.

Legal Briefs

Murder—An unlawful killing with malice aforethought.

Malice aforethought—Does not mean ill will or hatred; does mean the defendant had one of the following mental states:

1. intent to kill
2. intent to inflict great bodily harm
3. extreme recklessness/depraved indifference to whether the victim lived
4. intent to commit a felony

Felony murder rule—Generally, any death during the commission of a felony is murder. In some states, only certain dangerous felonies qualify, and states often place temporal and causation limitations on the rule's applicability.

Motive—Refers to the defendant's reason for committing the crime. While it may be considered evidence that the defendant did the crime, it is not something the prosecution is required to demonstrate in order to prove guilt.

Degree of murder—Generally speaking, killing by means of lying in wait, poison, bomb, torture, or during the course of certain violent felonies (such as arson, burglary, rape, and robbery) is first-degree murder.

1. In addition, most states provide that murders that are "willful, deliberate, and premeditated" are first-degree. All other murders are second-degree.
2. Some states instead rely on a set of aggravating and mitigating factors when determining punishment for a murder.

Chapter 5

⚖️

Voluntary Manslaughter

Q: When is an unlawful killing not murder?

A: When the victim is a lawyer.

No, not really. The correct answer is, when it's manslaughter. If a killing that would otherwise be murder is committed *in response to sufficient provocation*, it is voluntary manslaughter and is usually punished less severely than murder. If the killer acted with one of the states of mind necessary for malice aforethought (intent to kill, intent to inflict great bodily harm, etc.), but also acted with "hot blood" in response to some incitement, the law treats the killing as a less serious offense against society. This is "heat of passion"–type killings—the "I lost my head for a minute" and "just reacted" kind of thing. The idea is that an unlawful killing is obviously wrong, but that we (and the law) recognize that people sometimes respond rashly under certain conditions.

Obviously most people who kill are motivated by *some* feeling of provocation, whether it's jealousy at another's success or anger over a business deal gone sour. But not all of what we think of as "provocations" in the ordinary sense of the word meets the *legal standard* of "sufficient provocation." The law isn't prepared to hand out lesser punishment just because someone is unusually sensitive to insults or had an especially bad day or is just generally violent.

The requirements of "sufficient provocation" in most states are that:

1. The provocation must be the type that would cause a "reasonable person" to lose control of her passions and;
2. The time between the provocation and the killing must not have been long enough for a "reasonable person" to cool off.

Note that we're not talking about how *this* defendant reacted to the provocation; we're talking about how a *reasonable person* would have reacted. Whenever you see the term "reasonable person" in a criminal law context, it is meant to signal an *objective* standard of judging behavior. Essentially this mythical "reasonable person" acts as we would want a sensible person in our society to act and provides a standard by which we can measure this particular defendant's actions.

You might wonder whether a truly reasonable person would, under any circumstances, lose control and kill someone. Although various courts have described this reasonable person differently, a good way to think of it is to conceptualize an ordinary person who, like everyone else, has a breaking point.

An issue that frequently arises is whether the reasonable person standard should incorporate any of *this* particular defendant's characteristics (such as age, level of intoxication, past experiences, etc.). A woman who has been abused as a child might well react differently to a physical confrontation than others would. In fact, that person sounds like someone to whom we could be sympathetic. Of course, most people will not be sympathetic to every person who "snaps"—consider a man whose racist attitudes cause him to become violently enraged during a dispute with an Asian immigrant.

Some courts say that the reasonable person should not be regarded as having any of the defendant's characteristics since this would undercut the objective nature of the test; other courts say that the reasonable person can be considered to have *some* of the defendant's characteristics but probably not any that show a reduced ability to control his passions. The truth is, it's difficult to fashion an objective standard for measuring the behavior society expects while at the same time being fair to a particular defendant. There's no formula that applies across the board, and different states come up with different definitions.

Provocation

Over time, most jurisdictions developed rules about what is sufficiently provocative to cause a reasonable person to lose control of his passions. The standard ones included things like a serious physical attack or a husband finding his wife committing adultery. Acts that were *not* considered provocative enough to reduce a killing to manslaughter were a husband *learning* about his wife's adultery and "mere words" (abusive language, insults regarding your mother's sexual history, etc). The modern trend is to expand somewhat the concept of sufficient provocation beyond these rigid categories. For example, in some states, a husband who *learns* of his wife's infidelity and kills her may be guilty of manslaughter and not murder. And, of course, gender is no longer a factor; a wife who kills her husband's lover (or her husband) could likewise be found guilty of manslaughter.

Manslaughter is frequently an issue where there has been a killing in response to some type of physical assault. Not surprisingly, a minor assault will not be considered the type of provocation that brings about a "killing passion" in a reasonable person. So, it's not manslaughter if you shoot someone for pushing ahead of you in line at Starbucks. But a very violent attack could definitely be the trigger that reduces a killing from murder to manslaughter.

MUTUAL COMBAT

Generally, if two people agree to fight ("Hey, you wanna take this outside, buddy?") and one of them is killed, the crime is manslaughter, not murder. It doesn't really matter who threw the first punch because the "sufficient provocation" is the combat itself. Of course, there would have to be evidence that both participants agreed to fight; if a defendant simply issued the invitation and then clubbed the other guy over the head with a baseball bat, it's murder. The law isn't going to give you a lesser punishment just because you were clever enough to voice an offer immediately before butchering the object of your anger.

In a 2003 case that made national headlines because of issues of race and educational background, Harvard graduate student Alexander Pring-Wilson was convicted of manslaughter in the stabbing death of nineteen-year-old cook Michael Colono. Although the DA pushed for a murder conviction based on the theory that Pring-Wilson stabbed Colono in a street fight because he was angry at Colono for mocking him for being drunk, the jury apparently accepted Pring-Wilson's claim that he stabbed Colono in response to being brutally attacked by Colono and his cousin.

A key point to remember regarding provocation is that the defendant must prove not only that a reasonable person would have lost control, but that *he actually did lose control*. A killing won't be reduced to manslaughter where there is overwhelming evidence that a reasonable person would have lost control of her passion, but the evidence also shows that the defendant actually reacted in a cool and detached manner. If someone had overheard Pring-Wilson exclaim, "Even though I could easily stop this vicious attack using some simple self-defense moves taught to me by an ancient Tibetan monk, I think I'll just stab this fellow several times!" he would not have met the test for manslaughter.

Cooling Off Period

In the opening scene of episode #32 of *Close to Home*, Bob and Maxine Peters watch as David Hopkins, the man accused of killing their daughter, is found not guilty by a jury. Half an hour later, as Hopkins is giving media interviews on the steps of the courthouse, Bob Peters rushes toward him, firing a handgun. Unfortunately, Bob's aim is bad and instead of killing Hopkins, he kills one of Hopkins's lawyers and wounds another. He is immediately wrestled to the ground and arrested.

Annabeth Chase and the Indianapolis DA's office charge first-degree murder and want the death penalty. Hopkins's lawyer argues for voluntary manslaughter, saying that the shock of the not guilty verdict caused her client to act in the heat of passion. Annabeth, citing the fact that Peters brought the gun to the courthouse in his car and had nearly half an hour after the reading of the verdict to consider his actions, is reluctant to agree to voluntary manslaughter.

Eventually Peters is allowed to plead to voluntary manslaughter, in part because his lawyer was able to show that the assistant DA who tried the Hopkins murder may have unduly raised the Peters's expectations of a conviction, which may indeed have caused him to lose control of his emotions.

This scenario nicely frames the issue: since the whole idea underlying manslaughter is that the killer acted in the heat of passion, it only makes sense that manslaughter not apply if a reasonable person would have had time to "cool off" and regain control of his senses prior to the killing. Again, this is a "reasonable person" objective test; the focus is on whether an ordinary person of average temperament would have had time to calm down before killing the victim.

The obvious question here is also a difficult one to answer—how much time does it take for a reasonable person to cool off after a serious provocation? Courts struggle with this issue all the time and come up with different answers.

If an auto mechanic angrily confronts a customer over an unpaid bill and pushes the customer into a wall, after which the customer kills the mechanic by pushing him through a plate-glass window, is it manslaughter? Perhaps; we can imagine an ordinary person becoming so angered during a physical confrontation that they strike out with deadly force. But what if the customer goes home after the fight and stews overnight, then finds the mechanic the next day and unloads a shotgun in his face? It is difficult to see how an ordinary person wouldn't be able to regain his self-control overnight.

Now change the scenario. Instead of an argument that turns into a brawl, imagine a father learns that a neighbor has been abusing the father's young son and that after an agonizing night the father finds and kills the neighbor. Could news that shocking provoke an average person such that his passions could be "hot" hours, even days, after learning the truth? It's probably a much closer call than with the argument over the mechanic's bill.

TRANSLATIONS

Just to remind you that crime knows no borders, here are some translations for "manslaughter":

Danish: drab, manddrab
Dutch: doodslag
French: homicide involontaire
German: totschlag
Italian: omicidio colposo
Portugese: homicidio culposo
Spanish: homicidio involuntario

Legal Briefs

Voluntary manslaughter—a killing in response to "sufficient provocation" (a "heat of passion" killing).

Reasonable person—a mythical, always sensible person who acts and reacts exactly as we would like the average citizen to act.

Sufficient provocation—a legal standard; provocation that would make a "reasonable person" lose control of his emotions.

Cooling off period—the time between a provocation and a killing; if it is a long enough time for a reasonable person to regain control of her emotions, the killing (even if in response to legally sufficient provocation) is *not* voluntary manslaughter.

Chapter 6 ⚖

Involuntary Manslaughter

The final category of criminal homicide is involuntary manslaughter. Involuntary manslaughter is an *unintentional* killing resulting from (1) any act—even a lawful one—done in a criminally negligent manner; or (2) an unlawful act that is a misdemeanor or low-level felony. The main distinction between involuntary and voluntary manslaughter is that with involuntary manslaughter the death is *not* intended.

Criminally Negligent

This is another one of those places in criminal law where things aren't crystal clear; courts come up with lots of different standards for judging whether an act was done in a criminally negligent manner. Most courts, though, try to fit "criminal negligence" (sometimes called "culpable negligence" or "gross negligence") between an upper and lower standard of negligence.

The upper standard is "reckless indifference." Recall that a killing resulting from "reckless indifference" to human life is one of the ways in which "malice aforethought" is found and murder is charged. This type of extreme carelessness means something like firing a gun into a crowd of people at a bus stop. The lower end of negligence is "civil negligence" (sometimes called "ordinary negligence"). This type of action is not criminal and, as the name implies, would result only in a civil suit where the person harmed sues the careless person for damages. An example of civil negligence would be causing an accident by not clearing your windshield of snow and ice before madly dashing to work in the morning. The bottom line—criminal negligence is something *less* than "reckless indifference" and *more* than "civil negligence."

Episode #58 of the CBS series *Cold Case* illustrates the degree of negligence that can lead to involuntary manslaughter charges. In that show, Lily Rush of the Philadelphia cold case squad reopens a case that had been ruled a suicide. A dozen years earlier, high school student Trevor Dawson fell from the roof of his school. With no evidence of foul play, the police originally concluded that Trevor jumped to his death.

When a newly discovered note shows up (which happens with eerie frequency on this show), Rush reexamines the case and finds that while Trevor had actually made a suicide pact with other teenagers, he didn't kill himself. He and a classmate named Boris had planned to kill the abusive father of Trevor's girlfriend and then commit suicide, but when it came to it neither boy could bring himself to kill the father.

Upset, the boys went to the roof of their high school where Trevor revealed his newfound will to live so that he could still be with his girlfriend. When Boris, still planning to go through with the suicide pact, stepped to the edge of the roof, Trevor rushed to try to stop him from jumping. The two boys struggled on the ledge and Trevor fell to his death. When the truth becomes known (through those cool *Cold Case* flashback sequences), the now-adult Boris is charged with involuntary manslaughter.

The basis for the charge is that Boris created a dangerous situation by engaging in a physical struggle at the edge of a roof and that Trevor was killed as a result. If Boris had stepped away from the edge or simply not fought when Trevor tried to come to his aid, Trevor would not have died.

STATUTE OF LIMITATIONS

All states and the federal government have statutes that establish a time limit for prosecuting a crime (there are also time limitations for filing civil suits). The basis for a statute of limitations is simple fairness; over time, witnesses may die or their memories may fade, evidence can be lost, people want to move on with their lives, etc. Some crimes (such as murder) are considered to be so injurious to society that there are usually no limitations on when a prosecution can commence.

A *Dateline NBC* episode aptly named "Unfinished Business" focused on a 1997 quadruple murder in Polk County, Florida. The show portrayed the nearly five-year investigation that resulted in Nelson Serrano standing trial in 2006 for the murders of his former business partner and three other people connected to Serrano's former business. He was ultimately found guilty, and the jury recommended the death sentence.

Sometimes the cases can be even much older than nine years. Kennedy relative Michael Skakel appealed his conviction for the 1975 murder of Martha Moxley, saying that Connecticut's five-year statute of limitations on murder had expired by the time he was charged in 2000. The state high court ruled that when Connecticut eliminated the statute of limitations for murder in 1976, the change applied to Skakel's case, and the court upheld the conviction.

A man who sexually assaulted a student at the University of Virginia in 1984 and apologized to her in a 2005 letter as part of his Alcoholics Anonymous program pled guilty to aggravated sexual battery in 2006 and received a sentence of ten years, with all but eighteen months suspended. Virginia does not have a statute of limitations for felonies.

A real-life case of involuntary manslaughter is the infamous "dog-mauling" case from San Francisco. On January 26, 2001, Diane Whipple was chased down, mauled, and killed by two large dogs in the hallway outside of her apartment. The dogs (a 120-pound male and a 113-pound female, each heavier than the 110-pound Whipple) were raised as part of a dogfighting ring run from Pelican Bay State Prison by two inmates. The dogs were owned by Whipple's neighbors, couple Marjorie Knoller and Robert Noel, and it was Knoller who was unable to control the dogs when they attacked Whipple (Noel was not present during the attack).

The involuntary manslaughter charges were based on the theory that the couple knew the dogs were dangerous to others and did not take sufficient measures to safeguard the public from such threatening animals. There was evidence at trial that the couple knew the dogs were clearly dangerous; one acquaintance testified that the couple didn't even apologize after he was viciously bitten by one of the dogs. San Francisco assistant district attorney James Hammer explained it this way: "You knew it was dangerous and you did it anyway."

Law & Order aired an episode "inspired" by this same incident. In episode # 243, a woman and her small dog taking a walk in the park are killed by a pit bull that had been trained to fight. As in the real-life case, the dog was owned by the lawyer for an inmate (in Attica, not Pelican Bay) who ran a dogfighting business from prison. McCoy and Sutherlyn compared the pit bull to a "loaded gun" waiting to go off and argued that reckless handling of the dog (or gun) by not taking steps to protect the public was the basis for the involuntary manslaughter charge. The owners eventually pled guilty.

Misdemeanor or Low-Level Felony

Remember "felony-murder"? Well, this second type of involuntary man-slaughter is "felony-murder–lite." As with felony-murder, the unintentional killing occurs during the commission of an illegal act, but in this case a misdemeanor. This is sometimes even referred to as "misdemeanor-manslaughter." In addition, if the unintentional death occurs during a felony that does not qualify for the felony-murder rule, misdemeanor-manslaughter can be charged (which makes the term "misdemeanor-manslaughter" inaccurate, but it has a nice alliterative element to it and it's easy to remember, so it sticks).

Daniel Biechele, former tour manager for the band Great White, pleaded guilty to, among other things, 100 counts of misdemeanor manslaughter for his role in one of the nation's most devastating nightclub fires. Biechele admitted that in February 2003, he set off pyrotechnics at the Station night-club in West Warwick, Rhode Island, without a permit or license, uninten-tionally resulting in a massive blaze that destroyed the nightclub, killed 100 people, and injured 200 more. E-mail evidence showed that Biechele had been made aware of state-by-state laws requiring permits, and in some cases, authorized personnel to control the devices.

Some states limit misdemeanor manslaughter to cases where the un-lawful act is *malum in se* (wrong in itself) and will not charge involuntary manslaughter where the killing results from an act that is *malum prohibitum* (wrong because it is prohibited). When they break out the Latin, you know the law-types are getting serious. But understanding the difference between the two helps underscore the distinction between morality and law.

Murder is the classic example of something *malum in se*. Unlawful kill-ing is evil in itself; it is universally understood to be inherently wrong. On the other hand, something like ignoring a traffic light is wrong only be-cause there's a written statute that says so. So, causing an unintentional death by running a stop sign might *not* result in a charge of misdemeanor manslaughter.

Motor Vehicle Homicide

Most modern state criminal codes actually create a separate offense for death caused by the negligent operation of a motor vehicle or by operating a motor vehicle in an unlawful manner. The penalties for this "new" type of manslaughter are usually less severe than for traditional types of manslaughter.

Legal Briefs

Involuntary manslaughter—an *unintentional* killing resulting from a criminally negligent act or a misdemeanor (sometimes even a low-level felony).

Criminally negligent—does not meet the standard of "reckless indifference" to human life (firing a gun into a crowd) but is *more* than civil negligence (causing an accident by failing to clear your driveway of snow).

Misdemeanor manslaughter—a killing that occurs during a misdemeanor (in some states, also a low-level felony); "felony-murder-lite."

Chapter 7 ⚖

Rape

Rape laws have changed a great deal in response to society's evolving views on sex, equality, and even marriage. Nevertheless, rape is one of the most controversial areas of criminal law and seemingly every aspect of this crime, from its basic elements to data about how often it occurs, can trigger highly emotional debates. High-profile real-life cases easily capture the public's attention, and rape in its various guises is a popular and prominent issue in many TV law dramas (and even a principle theme of one—*Law & Order: SVU*).

Rape is commonly defined as unlawful sexual intercourse with a female person without her consent. There is a distinction between "forcible rape" (where intercourse comes about because of violence or threats), and "statutory rape" (where consent is given but is legally irrelevant because of the victim's age).

Forcible Rape

Traditionally, forcible rape required proof that the female did not consent to the intercourse *and* that the intercourse was accomplished by force (the meaning of "intercourse" is usually held to be the slightest vaginal penetration). Note that even where consent was lacking, there was no rape unless force was used. Typically, of course, the issues of force and consent are intertwined; evidence of force is usually sufficient to prove lack of consent (why else would force be necessary?).

There are those who argue that we should completely do away with the requirement that use of force be proved and that the victim's lack of consent should be the only relevant issue. The issue becomes, though, how to prove lack of consent where there is no showing that force was employed by the defendant.

By the Numbers

The FBI's *Crime in the United States, 2005,* shows that the number of forcible rapes known to the police in 1960 was 17,190 and in 2005 was *over* 93,000. There are many reasons (embarrassment, the perpetrator is a friend or family member, etc.) that likely cause rape to be an under-reported crime. Nevertheless, one interpretation of the data is that victims have felt increasingly comfortable reporting rapes since 1960.

Traditional rape law also required that the victim resisted the man's efforts with all her strength or "to the utmost" unless it was obvious that resistance would be overcome by force (a knife to the throat, gun to the head). The idea was that this would plainly demonstrate the victim's lack of consent. Just as obviously though, this requirement overlooks the fact that not all persons are equipped physically or psychologically to "fight back," and also that this approach runs the real risk of requiring victims to escalate the intensity of the perpetrator's violence. Thankfully, this requirement is no longer prevalent. Where it does still exist, the trend is to reduce its significance and only require a showing of some resistance to make clear that there was no consent to the intercourse.

Marital Immunity

The old rule was that a husband could not be guilty of rape of his lawful wife, even if he compelled his wife to submit to intercourse. The concept was rooted in the historic view that a wife was the "property" of the husband and that he had unfettered access to her. There was also a sense that by agreeing to the marital contract, the wife had permanently and irrevocably granted her consent to sexual intercourse with her husband. Most states have abolished or significantly modified this rule.

In some cases the victim may "consent" after the defendant places her in fear of imminent bodily harm. This "consent" is not legally valid and the perpetrator may be prosecuted for rape.

In still other cases, a victim may be *incapable* of giving consent—because of intoxication or insanity. Any intercourse with a female who is incapable of giving consent is rape, even if she somehow said words that indicated consent. An episode of Dominick Dunne's *Power, Privilege and Justice* called "Evil Deeds" dealing with the rape trial of Andrew Luster illustrates this concept.

Luster was heir to the Max Factor makeup fortune and lived off his trust funds on the beaches of California. Besides being an outdoorsman, he also lured women as young as sixteen to his home, plied them with alcohol and drugs (including the "date rape drug" GBH), and raped them. Because Luster was not only morally bankrupt but stupid as well, he videotaped some of these encounters. After his arrest in July 2000, the police found several of his tapes, including one labeled "Shauna GBHing." It was starkly clear from the tapes that the women were unconscious and therefore not able to give consent to intercourse. Shockingly, he was convicted of various counts of rape.

LUSTER'S LONG JOURNEY

Prior to and during his trial, Luster was free on a bail of $1 million (which had been reduced from the original $10 million bail). He was under house arrest and being monitored by an electronic ankle bracelet. During the Christmas break in the trial, Luster apparently sensed that things weren't going his way and cut off his ankle monitor and fled. Luster was convicted while absent from the trial (*in absentia*) and sentenced to 124 years in prison. In an interesting bit of television synergy, he was actually captured in Mexico by Duane "Dog" Chapman, who parlayed his notoriety into his own show on A&E creatively called *Dog the Bounty Hunter*.

"Dog" was himself arrested in September 2006, in Hawaii, and charged with illegal detention and conspiracy regarding his alleged kidnapping of Luster in Mexico in 2003 (he refused to turn Luster over to the Mexican authorities). "Dog" was initially arrested in Mexico on the charges, but never returned after posting bail in 2003. How ironic.

A *Law & Order: SVU* episode called "Obscene" (#119) focuses on the same point. In that show, a sixteen-year-old fan of shock-jock B. J. Cameron sneaks into the trailer of teenage television star Jessie Dawning to steal a pair of her panties. When he gets there, the young fan finds the starlet passed out on the couch after a long day on the set and a few too many painkillers. What starts out as a prank involving a glorified panty raid turns into rape as the fan discovers that Jessie is unresponsive. He begins to have sex with her, only stopping and fleeing when she begins to stir to wakefulness. This fictional rapist is no smarter than Andrew Luster, since he e-mails pictures of his encounter to his favorite shock-jock, who in turn gives them to Detective Stabler and ADA Novak. The fan eventually pleads guilty to the rape.

Being a smooth talker does not make someone a rapist. If a defendant seduces a female by convincing her that he is Brad Pitt or that having sex with him will be beneficial to her health, he cannot be convicted of rape. In these cases, the female consented to the act of intercourse, and "fraud in the inducement" is not punishable. However, if the defendant led the victim to believe that she was consenting to something other than intercourse, this is known as "fraud in the factum" and can be the basis for a rape conviction.

What about situations where the defendant believed that the female had given consent? The basic rule is that where the defendant *genuinely and reasonably* believes the female has given consent, he is not guilty of rape; "reasonably" means that there is an objective basis for the belief, not simply that the defendant subjectively held the belief. Obviously if the defendant used force or threats of violence, it would be difficult for him to claim that he believed there was consent.

An especially controversial aspect of rape law has been "rape-shield laws" enacted by most states, which limit the evidence that the defense can introduce in a rape trial. The purpose of these laws is to prevent the defendant from putting the victim on trial, as it were. Evidence about prior consensual sex with *the defendant* is generally admissible under these statutes; after all, if the defendant contends that the victim consented, her consent on another occasion is relevant, although not dispositive.

It's only when the defense tries to introduce evidence about the victim's *sexual history* with others or her *general reputation for chastity* that the shield laws come into play. Generally, this type of evidence will not be allowed, and the defense will not be able to cross-examine the victim about her sexual past. While this approach protects victims, it also has an impact on the defendant's right to confront his accuser and on his overall defense. Nevertheless, most states have decided that the benefits of the rape-shield laws outweigh the costs.

By the Numbers

According to the FBI's *Crime in the United States, 2005*, in 2005 law enforcement agencies across the nation cleared 41 percent of reported forcible rapes (a case is cleared when an arrest is made or when some element beyond the control of law enforcement prevented the police from making an arrest they otherwise would have made—a witness refuses to cooperate, dies, etc.).

SEXUAL ASSAULT

Many states have replaced the traditional crime of rape with an offense called "sexual assault" or something similar. These statutes are often gender-neutral and generally make punishable nonconsensual sexual conduct other than vaginal penetration (anal penetration, fellatio, cunnilingus, etc.).

Although less common, men are also the victims of rape. Episode #177 of *Law & Order: SVU* called "Philadelphia" dealt in part with two brothers who were pulling random men into a van from the streets of Central Park and raping them as a form of twisted revenge for the repeated rapes one of the brothers suffered while in prison. The rest of the episode revolved around Olivia finding her half brother, whose father had raped her mother. The half brother, Simon Marsden, is eventually arrested on charges of stalking and rape. That's quite a spectrum of rape cases for one episode, even *SVU*.

Statutory Rape

In most states, intercourse with a female under the age of consent is rape, without regard to whether she consented or whether any force, threats, or fraud was used. The "age of consent" varies from state to state, but is commonly somewhere in the sixteen to eighteen-year-old age range.

Statutory rape is a "strict liability offense," so the defendant doesn't even have to be aware of the victim's age. In fact, even if he has a good faith, reasonable belief that she is above the age of consent, he is still guilty of statutory rape. Claims that "she told me she was nineteen" or "her ID said she was twenty-one" are irrelevant; the man (or woman in the case of an underage male, in most states) is a rapist in the eyes of the law.

The sixteen-year-old member of a fundamentalist Mormon group testified to an Arizona grand jury that she had been raped twice by a man twelve years older than her who had taken her as his second wife. She testified that she told the man that she didn't want to have children, but that he forced her to have sex with him anyway. Nevertheless, the girl later refused to assist in the rape prosecution, perhaps in part due to the hold held over her by the group and its leader Warren Jeffs. The county attorney, however, insisted on going forward with statutory rape charges, known in Arizona as "sexual contact with a minor."

Perhaps the best-known case of statutory rape involves Joey Buttafuoco, whose seventeen-year-old lover shot his wife in the face in 1992.

Whether the "Long Island Lolita," as Amy Fisher was dubbed, gave consent to her sexual liaisons with Buttafuoco was irrelevant, and after pleading guilty to statutory rape, Buttafuoco served four months in prison. Fisher wound up serving seven years for the shooting. Amazingly, Buttafuoco and his wife remained married after the shooting. Hey, nothing says "I love you" more than causing someone to be shot in the face (they did divorce later). Of course, those who keep a close eye on the infamous Buttafuoco know that he has subsequently served time for insurance fraud and illegally possessing ammunition. In 2007, Buttofuoco and Fisher were seen together on a "date." True love never dies.

Legal Briefs

Rape—sometimes now called "sexual assault"; unlawful sexual intercourse or contact with a person without consent.

Forcible rape—a rape accomplished by force; generally there is no longer a requirement that the victim demonstrate that she (or he) resisted to "the utmost."

Marital immunity—the now-discarded rule that a husband cannot be charged with the rape of his wife.

Fraud in the inducement—lies told to convince a person to do something, like consent to have sex; usually not criminal.

Sexual assault—a term created by modern statutes to update traditional rape laws; generally making the crime applicable to other forms of sexual assault and making the offense gender neutral.

Statutory rape—a strict liability offense of having sexual relations with a victim under the age of consent (usually sixteen); the victim's consent is irrelevant.

Chapter 8   ⚖

Assault

What would happen if you bit your girlfriend several times on her back, or struck a police officer who was trying to stop your friend from commandeering a police horse, or threw a phone at a hotel employee, or a dumped a bottle of whiskey over the head of a romantic rival? You would be charged with some form of assault. And that is what happened to the celebrities involved in these fracases (sports announcer Marv Albert making use of his famous mouth, country music star Tim McGraw trying to "rescue" the mounted Kenny Chesney, actor Russell Crowe with the phone manners of a two-year-old, and rock star Courtney Love having a problem holding her whiskey). You wouldn't get as much press coverage, though.

Of course, it's not just ill-mannered celebrities who commit assaults. Well before his famous midnight ride, Paul Revere was charged with assaulting and beating the husband of one of his cousins. In 1761, Revere was hauled into court, found guilty, and ordered to pay a fine. Probably not his finest hour, but in retrospect, it does seem to be a demonstration of the fighting spirit the young colonies would soon need.

Of all the crimes of violence, including homicide and rape, assault in its varying degrees is by far the most common. That shouldn't be too surprising; criminal assault covers a wide range of actual and threatened physical attacks, from a simple shove during a disagreement between harried holiday shoppers over a parking space to brutal attacks fueled by rage and often made worse by the use of weapons.

The term "assault" actually encompasses two separate traditional crimes—"battery" and "assault." The traditional crime of "battery" was the unlawful use of force on another (landing ye olde haymaker on the nose of another during the weekly tavern brawl). In fact, "battery" did not have to be anything as dramatic as a punch in the face; it used to be that almost any application of force to another, even without any injury, would suffice. The traditional crime of "assault" was an *attempt* to commit a battery (swinging your scythe at a farmer who wandered into your field, but missing).

BY THE NUMBERS

The *Criminal Victimization in the United States, 2005 Statistical Tables*, shows that there were 3,959,900 assaults in 2005. This included all unlawful physical attacks or threats of physical attacks. Excluded from this number were rapes, attempted rapes, sexual assaults, robberies, and attempted robberies. Of these nearly 4 million assaults, about 51 percent involved non-strangers, and 49 percent involved strangers (Table 63).

Although in some states the crime is still labeled "assault and battery," many states now use the term "assault" to cover both traditional crimes. No matter the terminology used, lawyers and judges still like to know whether the crime in question was a "battery" or an "assault."

"Battery-Type" Assault

Today, something more than the mere application of force (as in a light touching) is required. Statutes typically require either that the application of force cause some bodily injury or that the touching is of the type likely to be regarded as offensive. The bodily injury does not have to be a black eye or broken ribs—a Des Moines, Iowa, man was charged with domestic assault for tattooing his girlfriend's ankle while she slept (after she took a sleeping pill and painkiller).

"Offensive touching" is also a broad category but likely wouldn't include something like a pat on the back, since this is a socially acceptable behavior that is not likely to be regarded as offensive (even if the person receiving the pat on the back was somehow offended). However, actor Christian Slater was arrested in 2005 for grabbing a woman's buttocks as she walked by him in Manhattan at 2:00 a.m. While touching a stranger's buttocks without consent is a perfect example of an offensive touching, the contact does not have to be sexual in nature; anything that would be considered affronting or rude could fit. Offensive touching could even apply to things *on* the victim (removing someone's sunglasses during a confrontation).

GIRLS GONE WILD

Most people probably think of assault as a "male" crime, what with all the violence. For better or worse, though, girls are starting to catch up with boys in this area. From 1996 to 2005, the FBI's *Crime in the United States, 2005*, shows that the number of girls under the age of eighteen charged with assaults rose 24 percent, while the number of boys under the age of eighteen charged with assaults declined 4.1 percent (Table 33).

Generally, the mental state required for a battery type assault is *negligence*; a person can be found guilty of battery if she should have been aware that her conduct would result in the application of some force to another (and the conduct left some bodily injury or was likely to be considered offensive). Supermodel Naomi Campbell was charged with assault for hitting her maid with a cell phone in a dispute over a pair of missing jeans. When Campbell pled guilty in January 2007, she told the judge: "I threw the cell phone in the apartment. The cell phone hit Ana. This was an accident because I did not intend to hit her." Accident or not, her actions still met the minimum standard of negligence.

VIOLENCE IN SPORTS

What about sports where violent contact is part of the game (football or hockey) and sports where violence is the whole game (boxing, mixed-martial arts fights, etc.)? And what about other areas of life where your body is in some way damaged or at risk (surgery, dental work)? Commonly, courts recognize a defense of consent in these areas, especially where there is societal acceptance of the risks (sports) and where there is a clear benefit from the defendant's actions (surgeon). The consent must be given voluntarily and the person consenting must be legally capable of consenting—not so young as to be unable to evaluate and not someone intoxicated or with a mental abnormality. Consent might also be a defense to "mutual combat" assaults, as in episode #81 of *Cold Case* where Lilly, Danny, and Nick investigate members of a high-school "fight club."

In real life, violence in sports can lead to criminal prosecution. Even in the National Hockey League, where savage checking and fistfighting are commonplace, some things cross the line from sports to crime. In March 2007, New York Islanders forward Chris Simon was suspended for twenty-five games for a vicious two-hand stick attack to the face of New York Rangers Ryan Hollweg (yes, even in New York some things shock the conscience). Local prosecutors reviewed the case and, partly in consideration of Hollweg's wishes, declined to charge Simon with a crime, although they seemed to believe they could have.

Interestingly, battery-type assaults can also be accomplished by *indirect means* where the defendant initiates some force that touches the victim—as in poisoning someone. This can happen in any number of ways. An unusual example is the 2006 Michigan trial of a man charged with assault for allegedly rubbing a suspicious compound on his palm before shaking hands with the prosecutor, police officer, and courtroom bailiff at the conclusion of a trial at which he was convicted of driving without insurance. The prosecutor, officer, and bailiff all became ill after the handshakes. The touching charged in this case was not the handshake, which in itself is not harmful or offensive, but instead the introduction of the substance that caused the harm (the defendant was later acquitted of assault at trial).

Almost always battery-type assault, commonly referred to as "simple assault," is a misdemeanor. More serious assaults (often called "aggravated assaults") are felonies. Aggravated batteries include those that result in serious bodily harm to the victim, those committed with the intent to rape or kill, and those carried out by means of a dangerous or deadly weapon.

Episode #20 of *The Closer* entitled "Head Over Heels" gives an interesting example of the type of serious harm that makes an assault a felony. In that episode, a pornography company called "Opulence" discovered through its regular testing that one of its male stars was HIV positive. Nevertheless, in order not to lose his services, the owner of Opulence never told the star of his condition. When that star's head is later discovered in a dumpster, Deputy Police Chief Brenda Johnson is on the case.

She eventually uncovers the truth: the star learned the true status of his health and was outraged because he had unknowingly infected several women, including his wife. (He died in a confrontation with the owner's son, who subsequently dismembered the body and placed the head in the dumpster to make it look like a random killing.) When Johnson charges the owner of Opulence with "Assault to Commit Great Bodily Injury," she says: "It's like pointing a loaded gun at their heads." Johnson's point was that allowing the male star to have unprotected sex with dozens of women was an assault on the infected women by indirect means with a potentially deadly virus. Surely that deserves greater punishment than a punch in the nose.

INJURIES

Although most states require something more than the mere application of force (some slight touching) to make an assault, the majority of assault victims in 2005 did not suffer physical injury. According to the 2005 *Criminal Victimization in the United States, 2005 Statistical Tables,* only 25.8 percent of assault victims sustained physical injury (Table 75). In just over 70 percent of all assaults, no weapon was used, but in aggravated assaults where there was an injury, a weapon was used over 78 percent of the time (Table 66). (These figures do not include assaults during robberies or sexual assaults.)

Prosecutors generally have a great deal of leeway in deciding whether to charge a battery-type assault as a misdemeanor or a felony. A punch to the stomach is probably a misdemeanor, but if the defendant kicks the victim in the stomach, the prosecutor could decide to charge the incident as an aggravated (felony) assault with a dangerous weapon (the shod foot), even though the injuries might be the same or even worse with the punch. This explains why Tim McGraw was only charged with assault after his attack left a police officer with a herniated disk and Courtney Love was charged with *felony* assault for attacking a woman with a whiskey bottle and leaving only bruises, bumps, and a chipped tooth. The underlying principle is that society has an interest in deterring the use of weapons in assaults.

SAFE AT HOME?

While we'd all like to think of home as a place of comfort and security, the statistics say otherwise. According to the *Criminal Victimization in the United States, 2005 Statistical Tables,* nearly a quarter of all aggravated assaults occur in or near the victim's home. The next most likely place to suffer an aggravated assault? A friend's, relative's, or neighbor's home (Table 61).

"Assault-Type" Assault

In most modern statutory schemes, either an *attempt to commit a battery* or *intentionally placing someone in fear of a battery* is an assault.

With the *attempt to commit a battery assault,* it is important to realize that the mental state required is more than the intent to frighten; the defendant must have actually intended the application of some force. So, although negligence will suffice for a battery-assault (negligently tossing a car battery and injuring your fellow mechanic—a battery-by-battery assault), a more specific intent is required for an *attempt* to commit a battery. Some jurisdictions also require the "present ability to succeed" in order to convict on an attempted battery. In those states, if the defendant tries to shoot a victim with an unloaded gun, no assault has occurred.

"Intentionally Placing in Fear" Assault

This type of assault requires that the defendant take some action that would put a reasonable person in fear of imminent bodily harm. Note the "reasonable person" language; this is an *objective* standard, and even if this particular victim is the cowardly-lion–type, words usually won't be enough. However, threatening words coupled with a drawn knife would likely be enough to put any reasonable person in fear of harm. There must be some evidence that the victim was actually in fear; if the victim doesn't hear the threats or see the knife, there has been no assault.

Mayhem

While not technically an assault, mayhem is a closely related offense. Historically, the crime of mayhem required that the defendant maliciously deprive the victim of the use of his limbs, rendering him less able to fight. Subsequently, the definition of mayhem was expanded to cover other disfigurements. Today, states that still have the crime of mayhem usually define it as disfiguring another or disabling another by causing loss of use of a limb, tongue, nose, eye, or testicle. It is commonly a felony.

The disfigurement or disabling must be of the permanent variety. If the bone can be set easily or the sliced ear stitched up well enough, there is no mayhem. So, Mike Tyson probably did not commit mayhem when he bit off part of Evander Holyfield's ear during their 1997 heavyweight fight because the ear was reparable (although likely not to its original condition). Given the intense physical contact anticipated in professional boxing, Tyson probably didn't even commit an assault (although one could argue otherwise).

Mayhem used to be punished by mutilating the defendant in the same manner as the victim. That is no longer the case today, although if it were, it would probably make for some very popular reality TV shows.

Legal Briefs

Assault—covers both traditional crimes of battery (hitting) and assault (attempting to hit or placing in fear).

Offensive touching—any physical contact that is likely to be regarded as unwelcome (grabbing someone's buttocks).

Aggravated assault—a more serious assault resulting in significant physical harm; often involving a weapon (club, shoe, etc.); a felony.

Intentionally placing in fear—purposely placing someone in fear of a battery; sometimes the "present ability" to commit the battery is required; based on a "reasonable person" standard.

Mayhem—not technically an assault; maliciously depriving the victim of use of limbs, eyes, etc.; today usually expanded to cover disfiguring the victim.

Chapter 9 ⚖

Kidnapping

What makes Robert Louis Stevenson's classic coming-of-age novel *Kidnapped* the quintessential late-eighteenth-century kidnapping story? Yes, there's the title. More important, the story fits squarely within the traditional definition of kidnapping—the forcible abduction of a person from his own country and sending him to another. As you undoubtedly recall from high school, young Scottish lad David Balfour sets out to collect his rightful inheritance from his uncle, Ebenezer Balfour. Although Uncle Ebenezer initially takes David in, he then arranges to have David abducted and put on a slavery ship bound for America. Happily, everything comes up roses for David, who shares many adventures on his way home to claim what is rightfully his.

Today, kidnapping does not necessarily involve taking a person to another country; instead, kidnapping means *the confinement of a victim involving either moving the victim or concealing the victim in some type of secret place,* and is usually a felony.

FALSE IMPRISONMENT

Kidnapping is an aggravated form of a separate crime called *false imprisonment.* False imprisonment is the unlawful confinement of another without his consent (compelling a person to remain where he does not want to or making him go somewhere that he does not want to remain). The confinement must be intentional and the crime is generally a misdemeanor.

"Confinement" is defined as making a person go where she does not want to go or compelling her to remain where she does not want to remain.

The confinement may be accomplished by force, threats, or both; it's probably not enough to trick the victim into going or remaining somewhere (unless, perhaps the victim is a child or is mentally incompetent). The "secret place" doesn't have to be a bat cave hidden hundreds of feet below ground or an abandoned mining shack high in the mountains; it can be anyplace where it is unlikely that the victim will be found.

The amount of "movement" required for a kidnapping can vary from state to state. Some courts say that any movement suffices because it is the act of forcing the victim to move that should be the focus of the crime; other courts would hold that only some substantial forced movement warrants the felony punishment that kidnapping carries.

Meaning

Why is the word **kid**napping when the victim can be any age? When the term originated, the "kids" who were nabbed were not youngsters, but workers (called "kids"), who were recruited by force or trickery for service on American plantations (much like David Balfour in *Kidnapped*). The crime originally had more to do with adults than children (who were less likely to be of much use on a plantation). In fact, there actually used to be separate terms—*adult* kidnapping and *child* kidnapping—but they have merged in modern legal usage.

Before OJ Simpson, the trial-of-the-century was a kidnapping case; specifically the kidnapping of twenty-month-old Charles Lindbergh Jr. from his home on March 1, 1932. Although a $50,000 ransom was paid, the boy was found dead in the woods two miles from the Lindbergh home in May 1932. Obviously, taking a twenty-month-old for ransom meets the definition of kidnapping. Two years later Bruno Hauptmann was arrested and charged with the kidnapping and murder.

The charges were based on strong circumstantial evidence, including a handwriting analysis that matched Hauptmann's writing to the ransom notes. He was convicted and executed in 1935. Many have had lingering doubts about Hauptmann's guilt. He was after all a German at a time of heightened American fears about Germany's place in the world. Some have questioned the accuracy of the forensic science used as evidence against Hauptman.

To shed light on the case, in 2005, Court TV aired a documentary that reexamined the evidence (which has been preserved in a museum in New Jersey). Although not definitive, a fresh look at the evidence suggests that

Hauptmann was indeed guilty. For example, three renowned handwriting experts analyzed the ransom notes and all concluded that there was a high probability that Hauptman wrote the notes. Nevertheless, some people will likely never be convinced that justice was done in that case.

Some states treat kidnapping as a more serious felony if there are certain aggravating factors that make it a worse offense against society's norms. These factors are generally spelled out in the kidnapping statute and include things such as kidnapping for ransom, kidnapping for purposes of sexual assault, or kidnapping a child. The penalty for these forms of aggravated kidnapping is usually greater than for other kidnappings.

There is an interesting question here, though, that comes up when the kidnapping is part of another crime, such as robbery or rape. Is the defendant guilty of both crimes even where the kidnapping may have been only incidental to the crime? The general rule is that the defendant is only guilty of kidnapping if the forced movement or confinement substantially increased the risk to the victim beyond the risk necessarily created by the other crime.

WHO KIDNAPS KIDS?

According to the U.S. Department of Justice, Office of Juvenile Justice Delinquency Prevention Juvenile Justice Bulletin, June 2004, in 2000, 49 percent of kidnappings were by a relative of the victim, 27 percent were by an acquaintance of the victim, and 24 percent were by strangers to the victim.

Legal Briefs

Kidnapping—confinement of a person involving either moving the victim or concealing the victim in a secret place; accomplished by force, threats, or both.

Movement—varies by jurisdiction; some courts say any movement suffices, others require more substantial forced movement.

Secret place—any place where the victim is unlikely to be found; does not have to be an underground cave or cabin high in the mountains.

False imprisonment—unlawful confinement of a person without her consent (making the person remain where she does not wish to remain); usually a misdemeanor.

Chapter 10 ———————————— ⚖

Acquisition Offenses

Society doesn't much care if you steal a glance, steal someone's heart, or steal home plate, but stealing property is an entirely different matter. There are a variety of different ways to steal (snatching and fleeing, taking by force, obtaining title by fraud, etc.), and mainly because of tradition and historical accidents, there are a medley of crimes to cover these situations (larceny, robbery, false pretenses, etc.). Although all of these are *acquisition offenses* (involving the wrongful appropriation of property), each has distinct elements. In some cases the distinctions between them are slight and fairly technical. It likely doesn't make a bit of difference to the victim whether the offense is called "larceny" or "robbery"; if your wallet is stolen, you still need to cancel all your credit cards and hope like hell that whoever took it doesn't make house calls. But the law is a finicky creature, and the police and prosecutors have to examine carefully the elements of the various offenses to decide which crime (if any) to charge.

Larceny

Larceny is essentially interfering with someone's *possession* of property. This is your basic, garden-variety stealing, shoplifting, etc. It is often called "theft." The elements of larceny are:

1. a trespassory
2. taking and
3. carrying away
4. the personal property

5. of another

6. with the intent to permanently deprive the owner of possession.

"Trespassory" is the fancy lawyer word for wrongful, and here means without the consent of the victim; if the defendant has permission to take the property and keep it, there is no crime. What if the defendant tricks the victim into giving her permission to take possession of the property by a promise to return it even though the defendant has no intention of ever returning the "borrowed" property? This is commonly called "larceny by trick" and is still larceny as long as it can be shown that the defendant didn't intend to keep the promise at the time she made it. "Larceny by trick" also covers obtaining property by other deceptions.

The "taking" required for larceny means *exercising control* over the property. Usually, the "taking" element is part of the "carrying away" element, but sometimes there can be independent evidence of each. Actress Winona Ryder was arrested for shoplifting (and drug possession charges) outside of an upscale department store in December 2001. Video from the store's security cameras and testimony from store security officers showed Ryder taking merchandise worth over $5,000 into a dressing room and cutting off the store security tags with scissors. This by itself is evidence of "taking" since she was exercising control of the $1,500 Gucci dress and $80 pair of socks in a way incompatible with the store's ownership rights to the property. Of course, she then secreted the items in a bag and walked out of the store, evidence that satisfies both the taking and carrying away elements of the crime (which was a felony because of the value of the merchandise—states usually make stealing property worth less than a certain dollar amount a misdemeanor, anything above a felony).

The "personal property" of another" simply means that the defendant must have taken the property from someone else (including a store) who had possession of it. Bear in mind that we're talking about *possession*, not title, here. If you bring your car to a garage to be repaired and later drive off without paying, you may have committed larceny. The garage had a mechanic's lien on the car until payment is made and thus had *possession* of the car; the fact that you always had title to the car is irrelevant.

The definition of property is often expanded by statute to cover things like documents, records, and electronically stored data. In episode #20 of *Law & Order: Criminal Intent* entitled "Badge," Detectives Goren and Eames discover that a city auditor was murdered by ex-police officers who worked for a security service being audited by the city. As part of his standard incredibly clever plan to capture the bad-guys, Goren catches one of the ex-officers using a computer to try to steal a police file that would link her to the murder. When the police burst into the room, Goren informs the woman that she is being arrested in part for "larceny of a police file."

SATISFYING A DEBT

It is generally not larceny when someone takes property that she honestly believes she is entitled to as repayment of a debt. In that case the defendant sees the property as hers and therefore is not taking the property "of another." Of course, the property taken must not be of greater value than the debt that is believed to be owed.

"Intent to permanently deprive" means pretty much what it says, although it also covers cases where the defendant used the property in a way that involves a significant risk of loss to the owner (taking a car without permission and leaving it running on the street in a high-crime neighborhood).

If the defendant intends to return the property within a reasonable period of time (the meaning of "reasonable" varies by circumstances and the type of property), she has not committed larceny. However, many states have statutes specifically making it a crime to take a car for a "joyride" even if the car is returned to the owner.

BY THE NUMBERS

The *Criminal Victimization in the United States, 2005 Statistical Tables*, reveals that of the more than 13 million theft (larceny) offenses in 2005 (not including motor vehicle theft), almost 27 percent involved a loss of less than $50, and only 7.7 percent involved a loss of more than $1,000 (Table 83). In addition, there was total recovery of the stolen property in less than 5 percent of the cases, and some recovery of stolen property in 3.6 percent of the cases (Table 86).

Robbery

It's almost dawn, closing time for a neighborhood bar in New York City. The bartender and the bouncer are cleaning up for the night and as they turn on the neon "closed" sign, the bouncer heads toward the front door to lock it. Suddenly a man pushes his way through the door. He's wearing a green hooded sweatshirt that obscures his face and waving a gun around. He gets all the cash from the register and shoots the bartender twice before running off. In this episode of *CSI:NY* (# 58), Detective Flack seems to get it right when he describes the scene to Mac and Stella as a straight robbery (of course, in keeping with the *CSI* motif where nothing is as it first appears, the robbery eventually turns out to be a way to frame CSI member Hawkes).

Robbery is basically an aggravated form of larceny. It requires proof of all the elements of larceny *and* two other elements:

1. the property must be taken from the victim's person or presence
2. the taking must be accomplished by violence or intimidation. (You can see why this is an aggravated form of larceny. When the guy wearing the bandana around his face puts a gun to your back and demands "all your money," it is much more unsettling than when a pickpocket relieves you of your wallet in a crowd—larceny. As in our *CSI* example, the violence involved in a robbery can quickly turn a bad situation into a deadly one.)

"Taken from the victim's person" is straightforward. The victim's "presence" means things the victim controls within his vicinity. If the victim is at home, all the rooms in his house are within his presence. Also, the cash register at a store is within the employee's presence even if she is forced into a back room or closet.

Episode #38 of *NUMB3RS* helps clarify this point about the "presence" of the victim. In that show, thirty-year-old teacher Crystal Hoyt and her seventeen-year-old boyfriend Buck are on a savage seven-state crime spree heading to California. At one point, nearly out of money and gas, they pull into a small roadside diner in the middle of nowhere. Crystal grabs her handgun, Buck his shotgun, and they brazenly walk into the diner waving the weapons. After Buck shoots a round into the ceiling, Crystal orders the only employee of the diner to open the register. She then shovels the cash into a bag while the employee crouches behind the counter. Although the money is not on his person or any person, Crystal and Buck are definitely robbing the diner (if the "employee" is the owner, it is his cash; if he's not the owner, he at least has lawful possession of the cash). Buck then demands that one of the customers hand over the keys to his BMW in the parking lot. Obviously the man was not physically in possession of the car as he sat in the booth, but it was still in his "presence," and Buck and Crystal clearly robbed him also. (Robbery was the least serious crime they committed because they also wound up shooting both the employee and the customers.)

The "violence" required for robbery is almost any force used to take the property. A pickpocket doesn't usually use force, but if the victim becomes aware of the pickpocket's efforts and struggles to keep possession of the wallet, it is now a robbery. Likewise, it is probably not robbery to snatch a purse or money out of a victim's hand so suddenly that no resistance is offered; however, if there is a tussle, it is robbery. Even the force needed to break a purse strap or the chain off a victim's neck can suffice for robbery (although the Model Penal Code restricts "robbery by violence" to instances where there is serious bodily injury).

SERVICE WITH A SMILE

The traditional advice to bank employees about how to react to a robber (don't approach, activate a silent alarm, etc.) may not be the best approach. The easiest way to foil a would-be bank robber may be something as simple as a smile and a friendly greeting. Extreme friendliness is the focus of the "Safecatch" system created by Seattle, Washington FBI Special Agent Larry Carr. The idea is that courtesy may unnerve the robber and cause him to rethink the crime and walk away. When a man walked into a branch last year wearing gardening gloves and sunglasses, the manager greeted him, invited him to remove the sunglasses, and brought him over to a very friendly teller. The man, who Agent Carr suspected was the "Garden Glove Bandit," simply asked for a roll of quarters and left.

Where intimidation is the basis for a robbery charge, the victim must have actually been in fear, the fear must have been caused by the defendant's actions, and that the fear must be objectively reasonable. The threat involved generally must be of death, serious bodily injury, or deleting the 7,000 songs on someone's iPod (*worse* than death to some people).

An implied threat, like waving a weapon or even a fist in the victim's face, is probably even enough. After leading Ohio State to the national championship in 2002, football star Maurice Clarett pled guilty to a robbery charge after he was arrested for flashing a gun at two people and taking a cell phone from them.

INJURY ON TOP OF INSULT

Bad enough to lose your property, but it hurts a little more when you suffer a physical injury as well. In 2005, of the more than 415,000 completed robberies, the *Criminal Victimization in the United States, 2005 Statistical Tables*, shows that over 140,000 of them resulted in injury to the victim (Table 7).

Embezzlement

Embezzlement requires that the following elements be shown:

1. The fraudulent
2. conversion
3. of property
4. of another
5. by a person in lawful possession of that property. (Embezzlement is distinguished from larceny in that the misappropriation of the property occurs *while the defendant has lawful possession* of the property, while larceny involves the defendant unlawfully obtaining possession of the property.)

The classic embezzlement case involves the bookkeeper at a business siphoning off money that she should deposit in the business's account (so it's money that she *lawfully has possession of*—although her job requires her to deposit the money in the business's account) and using it to fund her own lifestyle, whatever that might be. For example, in a 2007 case that attracted national attention, the bookkeeper for J & J Materials in Massachusetts pled guilty to embezzling $6.9 million that she used to buy a ranch in Vermont, a life-size statue of Al Capone, a private performance by Burt Bacharach, six talking trees modeled after the "Wizard of Oz" characters, and more than thirty-five vehicles. Now, how was she supposed to afford all that on her $40,000-a-year salary? And why did no one notice her lavish lifestyle over the six years that she embezzled the money?

Perhaps an even more startling case of embezzlement came from California, where in 2007 a pastor pled guilty to embezzlement after he *stole a church*. Seriously, Randall Radic, pastor at First Congregational Baptist Church in Ripon, sold the property where he worked. First, he faked documents giving him ownership of the parsonage, and then used the property to take out approximately $200,000 in personal loans. Then he forged papers giving him the power to sell the church he was in charge of, and he sold it for $525,000. Things began to turn when someone at a town bank called the church board and told them that Pastor Radic had just purchased a $102,000 BMW. The church eventually got its title back.

"Conversion" means a substantial and serious interference with the owner's rights to the property. "Taking" and "moving" the property usually won't be sufficient because in these situations the defendant has lawful possession of the property and probably has the authority to move the property. Basically, "conversion" requires some use of the property that is inconsistent with the agreement under which the defendant has possession of the property. While the mechanic at an automobile dealership may lawfully possess and use the dealership's tools while at work, it would be embezzlement if he decided to take some tools home. The conversion must also be "fraudulent," which is similar to larceny's "intent to permanently deprive"; if the mechanic intends to return the tools, he is probably not guilty of embezzlement. However, he must return the *exact* tools taken, not similar ones, or else he has committed embezzlement.

As with larceny, if the defendant converted the property to satisfy a debt she honestly believes she is owed, there is no crime.

Receiving Stolen Property

Receiving stolen property is exactly what it sounds like:

1. receiving possession and control
2. of stolen property
3. known to have been stolen
4. with the intent to permanently deprive the owner of her interest in the property.

Actually possessing the property suffices, but so does having the thief put the property in a place that the defendant chooses. A major issue in this crime revolves around the "known to be stolen" requirement. The defendant doesn't have to witness the theft; if he has reason to believe that property is stolen (being offered a giant plasma television for $200 by "Sticky Fingers Freddy" for example), that may be enough.

False Pretenses

"False pretenses" consists of:

1. obtaining title
2. to the property of another
3. by an intentional false statement of past or existing fact
4. with the intent to defraud.

This crime is distinguished from "larceny by trick" in that what is obtained by the false statement is *title* and not merely possession—think car dealer giving title to a car in exchange for a forged note. And on the subject of car dealers, an important limitation on the misrepresentation required for false pretenses is that the defendant must have created a false impression as to a matter of *fact*; mere "puffing" or expressing an opinion does not count (or pretty much every used car sale would be a crime). Also, the misrepresentation must be of a past or existing fact; a false promise regarding the future ("I promise I will get you the note by next week") is not sufficient.

Consolidation

Many states have combined larceny, embezzlement, false pretenses, and receiving stolen property into a single offense: theft. This makes it a lot easier on the police and prosecutors since they don't have to worry about charging the proper acquisition offense and being caught up in distinctions between "possession" and "title," etc. Robbery, which involves violence, is generally kept as a separate crime.

Legal Briefs

Larceny—a trespassory taking and carrying away the personal property of another with the intent to permanently deprive the owner of possession.

Robbery—an aggravated form of larceny; includes all the elements of larceny along with two additional elements—the property must be taken from the victim's person and the taking must be by violence or intimidation.

Embezzlement—the fraudulent conversion of property of another by a person in lawful possession of that property.

Conversion—a substantial interference with the owner's right to the property.

Receiving stolen property—receiving possession and control of property known to have been stolen.

False pretenses—obtaining title to the property of another with an intentional false statement of past or present fact with the intent to defraud.

Chapter 11 ⚖

Burglary

Burglary is one of the few crimes you see advertised. You don't see lots of TV commercials where citizens are being assaulted with dangerous weapons or kidnapped, but home security companies like ADT and Brinks spend a small fortune on commercials where we actually see the bad guys committing the crime (or at least trying to—those security systems never fail to save the day). The fact that corporate America puts so much money into advertising ways to prevent burglaries shows our determination to have our homes remain islands of safety in a frequently dangerous world.

The traditional definition of burglary was:

1. the breaking
2. and entering
3. of the dwelling of another
4. at nighttime
5. with the intent to commit a felony therein.

These elements were very technical, and sometimes the analyses had a "How many angels can dance on the head of a pin?" quality to them.

For example, "breaking" required the use of some force, but it was an open question as to how much force was necessary. Some courts said that opening a closed but unlocked door was sufficient; other courts said that even if the door was open six inches and the offender pushed it open slightly more to gain entry, this was a "breaking." The "breaking" had to have been to enter some part of the house—opening an unlocked closet door counted, but not smashing open a locked filing cabinet.

Modern statutes have generally recast the elements of burglary to make the definition of burglary more expansive. Often there is no requirement for "breaking"; any entry will suffice as long as it is unlawful or without consent. In addition, burglary is no longer confined to dwellings; nearly any structure can be involved. The "nighttime" element has also been kicked to the curb, and in most jurisdictions burglaries can (and unfortunately do) happen anytime, day or night.

Perhaps the most interesting element of burglary is the "intent to commit a felony therein." This remains an element in modern statutes, although it is sometime modified so that intent to commit a misdemeanor is sufficient. Basically, this means that *at the time of entry* the defendant must have *intended to commit a felony (or a misdemeanor)*. If the intent to commit the crime is formed after the entry to the building, there has not been a burglary. When someone enters a building to get out of the cold and *then* decides to steal some office equipment, there has been no burglary (although other charges such as unlawful entry and larceny might be warranted).

MODEL PENAL CODE

The Model Penal Code is more expansive than most state statutes. Under the MPC approach the intent to commit any crime, misdemeanor or felony, is sufficient for a burglary charge.

There is no requirement that the defendant actually complete (or even begin) the crime within the structure; all that is needed is the *intent*. In episode #17 of *Criminal Minds*, a court reporter turned vigilante is murdering people who have been acquitted by the criminal justice system. At one point he unlawfully enters the apartment of a woman and waits for her to return home before brutally killing her. Obviously he is guilty of murder, but he is also guilty of burglary the moment he enters the apartment with the intent to kill this woman.

Since the sole issue is the defendant's intent at the time of entry, the defendant has still committed a burglary if she abandons her criminal intent *after* entering; burglary is completed at the time the defendant enters the building with the requisite intent. Keeping this in mind, you can understand why in most states if a person actually completes the intended crime, she can be convicted of both burglary and the completed crime— they are separate criminal incidents. Our vigilante from *Criminal Minds* could have been convicted of both burglary and murder (if he hadn't been killed by a police sniper later in the episode).

BY THE NUMBERS

The FBI's *Crime in the United States, 2005*, shows that there were 2,154,126 million burglaries reported to the police in 2005. Of those, nearly two-thirds were burglaries of residences, and one-third were nonresidential structures. Most residential burglaries occurred during the daytime (6:00 a.m. to 6:00 p.m.) (Table 23). The clearance rate for burglaries was 12.7 percent (Table 25).

While the enduring image of burglary is of stealthy entry into a home at night to make off with the family silverware and jewelry, the intended crime can be just about any felony (or in some states, a misdemeanor such as any theft). For example, the intent could be to cause an enormous national scandal, bring down a presidency, and cause the American public to become extraordinarily cynical about the political process. Okay, the Watergate burglars had smaller aims when they broke into the headquarters of the Democratic National Committee on June 17, 1972 (fixing illegal wiretaps was one of the actual goals), but anything can happen in the wacky world of crime.

The intended crime could be a sexual assault. Self-proclaimed prophet Brian Mitchell and his wife Wanda Barzee used a knife to cut open a window screen and gain entry into a home in Salt Lake City in 2002. They forced a young teen girl from her bedroom at knifepoint and made her walk several miles to a hidden campsite where they tried to sexually assault her. Elizabeth Smart was missing for nine months, and news of her abduction and eventual rescue were national news. Mitchell and Barzee were each charged with burglary, aggravated sexual assault, and aggravated kidnapping.

The intended crime could be one of violence. In August 2006, Jonathan Eddington, a lawyer in Bridgeport, Connecticut, allegedly burst through the screen window of his neighbor's house while carrying a knife and stabbed fifty-nine-year-old Barry James thirteen times, killing him. Apparently Eddington carried out the attack after having a conversation with his wife, who told him that she suspected James of molesting their two-year-old daughter. Moments after that conversation, Eddington picked up the knife and went to James's house. Eddington was charged with burglary and murder.

Burglary is commonly a felony offense, but some states divide burglary into degrees and assign more serious punishment for "aggravated" or "first-degree" burglary. These aggravated or first-degree burglaries commonly include instances involving an inhabited dwelling and assaults. This makes sense to most people. Burglary of an empty warehouse doesn't instill the same type of fear as does one where an occupied family home is violated and, obviously, carrying out an assault such as rape or murder is much more serious than carrying off a camera. Sometimes a burglary at night will also bring a harsher penalty.

Legal Briefs

Burglary—breaking and entering a building with the intent to commit a felony (sometimes any crime) within.

Intent to commit a felony—at the time of the unlawful entry, the defendant must have intended to commit a felony (sometimes any crime) within; the burglary is complete upon unlawful entry with the intent to commit the crime, regardless of whether the crime is actually begun or completed.

Chapter 12 $\quad$ ⚖

Arson

Political protest is part of the fabric of this society. We have a long and rich tradition of fiery protests, fiery speeches, and occasional real fires. Nothing gets your point across more directly than flames leaping from a building set against the dark night sky.

Imagine an environmental group deciding to protest urban encroachment on natural settings by burning the offending structures to the ground; one of their signature "actions" is to torch a ski resort in Utah. Suppose the protest group is called "Coyote" and that three true-believers travel to New York City to burn a building being constructed on the former site of a beloved community garden. The three activists, all college students, believe that the building is unoccupied and use gasoline to set a fire that tragically results in the death of a woman inside the building. Dramatic? You bet. In fact, a good enough story to be episode #261 of *Law & Order* called "The Fire This Time."

In the "ripped from the headlines" custom of *Law & Order*, the episode is based in part on real-life crimes. In 1998 the Earth Liberation Front (ELF) claimed responsibility for eight separate fires at a Vail ski resort that caused an estimated $12 million in damage. ELF said that it targeted Vail because it was encroaching into the habitat of the endangered lynx.

ECOTERRORISM

There have been other acts of ecoterrorism by ELF in recent years. One example is the 2001 firebombing of the University of Washington's horticulture center. ELF claimed responsibility, saying that the center's work on fast-growing hybrid poplar trees was an "ecological nightmare" for the diversity of native forests.

Traditionally, arson was the "malicious burning of the dwelling of another." As with murder, "malice" does not imply "ill will," but instead encompasses different mental states that must be shown:

1. Intent to burn,
2. Knowledge that the building would burn, or
3. Intent to create an obvious fire hazard.

Negligence is *not* one of the mental states, so an accidental fire caused by carelessness would not be arson. Also, it was arson only if you burned the dwelling of another; if you were entitled to possession of the property, you could not be charged with arson for torching it.

Much as with burglary, the elements were highly technical and difficult to apply. For example, "burning" meant that part of the home had to be consumed by fire—scorching or blackening by heat would not meet the requirement—although there did not have to be any significant damage to the dwelling; any "consuming" by fire would suffice. One person's "scorching" might be another's "charring," which is a type of consumption. Modern statutes have significantly modified the definition of arson.

Typically, today, the burning of structures other than a dwelling will be arson. Also, the technical analysis of "burning" is often discarded and the focus is on whether the defendant started the fire with the intent to destroy the structure. In our *Law & Order* example, the evidence at trial showed that the college students used an accelerant (gasoline) and started the fire in a spot designed to cause the most damage to the building. Obviously they meant to burn the building to the ground—and then plant a peace garden.

Lots of us think of arson as a crime of profit, where the owner of a failing business decides to torch her building and collect on the insurance money. In that case, the burning with the intent to defraud an insurer is often a separate crime itself, although closely related to the facts and evidence of the underlying arson.

BY THE NUMBERS

According to the FBI's *Crime in the United States, 2005*, over 67,000 arson offenses were reported in 2005 (Table 12). Approximately 18 percent of those cases were cleared (Table 25).

Arson is commonly a felony offense. It is easy to understand why. Arson not only causes enormous physical and economic damage, it also puts innocent lives at risk, whether intentionally or not. As in our *Law & Order* example, a death from arson might be wholly unintentional, perhaps even unforeseeable, but the risk to firefighters and others is both real and obvious.

When a life is lost in an arson incident, the prosecution can usually charge felony-murder. While there is no "felony-murder-arson" rule, the basic principles of homicide law apply to this felony as well as any other.

Legal Briefs

Arson—the malicious burning of a structure; not an accidental burning; generally a felony.

Chapter 13 ⟵───────⟶ ⚖

Perjury

Losing your ethical compass is a common mishap, as every kid caught with a hand in the cookie jar can tell you. Thank goodness that your basic, garden-variety lie is not a criminal matter; Capitol Hill would be a mighty empty place, and most marriages would depend on conjugal visits. So, when *is* a lie a crime? When it offends the criminal justice system, that's when.

Perjury is willfully giving a false statement under oath in a judicial proceeding. Perjury is not confined to the courtroom; anytime the law authorizes the giving of an oath, perjury can apply (think of a legislative proceeding where a baseball player absolutely denies having used steroids, and subsequent testing casts significant doubt on the assertion—not that that would ever happen).

The "willful" part of the definition is important. It's not a crime to be mistaken, to guess, to speculate, or to shade the facts. If it were, just about every witness in the history of American trials would be guilty of perjury. The witness has to *know* the testimony she is giving is false and intentionally give the testimony under oath anyway.

This may be surprising, but not all lies under oath are perjury. Perjury applies only where the false statement is about a *material matter*. A "material matter" is something that could influence the outcome of the proceeding. So cutting a few years off your age probably wouldn't count, but falsely providing an alibi for a rapist surely would. It's not so much that the law considers it okay to lie sometimes, it's more that enormous amounts of time and resources could be spent chasing down every untruth, and it is wiser to concentrate on issues central to the proceeding.

What if a witness makes contradictory statements about a material fact in the same proceeding? Obvious perjury, right? One of the statements must be false. Well, in many jurisdictions, no. If the witness admits that one of the statements is not true, he is not guilty of perjury. The reason for this is purely practical—anything that gets to the truth of the matter is to be encouraged, so honestly copping to a lie in court is allowed.

Perjury cases are not exactly common, and they are often offshoots of other criminal matters. Take as an example the much-publicized case of the death of congressional intern Chandra Levy. U.S. Representative Gary Condit potentially exposed himself to perjury charges when he failed to admit to investigators until his third interview that he had had a romantic relationship with the missing twenty-four-year-old. Ultimately the issue was probably not material, and Condit was never charged with perjury.

Rapper Lil' Kim was charged with perjury in relation to a 2001 shootout in Manhattan between members of her entourage and those of a rival rapper. She was charged with lying during three separate appearances in front of the grand jury investigating the shootings. Although she was not a suspected shooter, investigators believed that she was lying about a material matter (whether a suspected shooter had been at the scene).

There is also a separate offense of "suborning perjury," which means inducing or causing someone else to commit perjury. Suborning perjury requires that the defendant: (1) know the testimony to be given is false, and (2) actually cause the witness to give false testimony under oath. Remember Monica Lewinsky? In a taped conversation, she said that she intended to lie in her deposition in the civil case involving President Clinton (where Paula Jones was suing him for sexual harassment). In that conversation, she also asked another witness to lie in a deposition. Saying that she intended to lie is not perjury, but asking a witness to lie could be suborning perjury.

Here's a curious issue for you; why isn't a defendant who takes the stand, proclaims his innocence, and is then convicted also charged with perjury? It's cut and dried—he took the stand, swore an oath, and knowingly gave testimony that has been proven in court to be false. Well, the truth is, everyone involved in the criminal justice system would see this as a huge waste of time that might also unconstitutionally inhibit a person's right to testify in her own defense.

Legal Briefs

Perjury—willfully giving a false statement under oath.

Material matter—something that could influence the outcome of the proceeding.

Suborning perjury—inducing someone else to commit perjury.

Chapter 14 ————————————— ⚖�

Solicitation

It is not a crime to think about committing a crime, but it *is* a crime to try to put that idea in someone else's head. This is called *solicitation*, and it refers to counseling or inciting someone else to commit a crime. Solicitation used to apply to counseling or inciting both misdemeanors and felonies, although sometimes today it applies only to serious felonies, like rape, murder, kidnapping, etc. The rationale behind punishing solicitation is that it is a danger to society when someone encourages another in a criminal enterprise. Society has a stake in trying to squelch criminal initiatives at the earliest possible moment.

Solicitation is a *specific intent crime*. The defendant must have intentionally encouraged another to commit a crime; it is *not* solicitation if you jokingly suggest that it would be great to steal your boss's Mercedes and your coworker takes the idea seriously (although chances are you'd both be fired).

The solicitation is complete once the defendant intentionally encourages or incites someone to commit a crime. The person doing the soliciting *does not have to do anything to help actually bring about the crime.* Further, the person solicited does not have to commit the crime, take any steps to commit the crime, or in fact even agree to commit the crime. The instant the exhortation to commit a crime is communicated, the crime is committed.

THE UNCOMMUNICATED SOLICITATION

What if a person writes a letter or sends an e-mail that is meant to incite another to commit a crime, say murder, but the letter or e-mail never reaches the intended party (the letter is lost, the e-mail is blocked by a firewall, etc.). Has a criminal solicitation been committed? Remember, the crime of solicitation is meant to punish those who make *an effort* to get someone to commit a crime. Does it make sense to determine criminal liability by the vagaries of the post office or the effectiveness of a firewall? As a point of reference, the Model Penal Code would call an uncommunicated solicitation a crime.

Soliciting prostitution is a well-known and common occurrence that brings to mind many colorful real-life incidents, but let's not get sidetracked on sports stars. Sometimes the crime solicited is one of violence. In 1991 a Texas woman was convicted of attempting to hire a hit man to kill the mother of her daughter's cheerleading rival. The plan was that the rival would be so upset by the death of her mother that she would be unable to qualify for a spot on the cheerleading team. The mother was convicted of soliciting capital murder.

MOVIE TIE-IN

The story of the murderously fierce cheerleading competition was so noteworthy that it spawned the movie called, no kidding: *The Positively True Adventures of the Alleged Cheerleader-Murdering Mom,* starring Holly Hunter (undoubtedly a high point of her career).

Actor Robert Blake of *Baretta* fame was charged both with the murder of his wife and soliciting her murder. Bonnie Lee Bakley was shot dead on May 4, 2001, as she sat in Blake's car near an Italian restaurant where they had just dined. Blake claimed that he returned briefly to the restaurant to retrieve his gun (not the gun used in the murder) and found his wife dead when he got back to the car. The prosecution contended that after failing to convince stuntman Ronald Hambleton to kill his wife, Blake did it himself.

The jury apparently did not find Hambleton credible (perhaps swayed by evidence of his history of drug-induced delusional behavior) and acquitted Blake on the charge of soliciting murder. They also acquitted Blake of the actual murder and deadlocked on a second charge of soliciting murder (which was eventually dismissed).

Solicitation is flexible enough to cover crimes other than prostitution and murder—nearly any crime will do (depending on the state) from shoplifting to kidnapping. In 2006 a youth-baseball coach was charged with trying to pay one of his players to hurt an autistic teammate so that the teammate couldn't play. The coach was eventually convicted of criminal solicitation to commit simple assault after the player testified that on the coach's instructions he threw baseballs at the autistic boy's groin and ear. That coach did not win the league's "coach of the year" award.

Traditionally, solicitation was punished to the same degree as the offense solicited. Modern statutes usually provide for a lesser penalty for the solicitation than for the crime contemplated.

MODEL PENAL CODE

The MPC approach is that soliciting the commission of any offense is a crime. Also, the Code would have the same penalty for the solicitation as for the offense solicited.

Legal Briefs

Solicitation—counseling or inciting another to commit a crime, usually a felony.

Uncommunicated solicitation—a solicitation that does not reach the intended person, blocked by a firewall, etc. As a point of reference, the Model Penal Code would call an uncommunicated solicitation a crime.

Chapter 15 ⚖

Conspiracy

Imagine that you are being prosecuted for a murder in Los Angeles but that the DA doesn't have to prove that you were even *in* Los Angeles when the murder occurred. How could that be? We only prosecute people when we have evidence that they committed the crime, right? Well, not exactly. Sometimes we prosecute people because, as moms have been saying for generations, they "got mixed up with the wrong crowd."

Prosecutors believed that in 1975, Sara Jane Olson drove with two friends from the Bay area to Los Angeles and planted a powerful explosive device under a pair of police cruisers. Neither bomb exploded. Nevertheless, in 1976, Olson was charged with conspiracy to commit murder.

All a jury needed to convict Olson was to find that she was one of a group plotting murder and that someone in the group, not necessarily her, took some concrete action to advance the plan. The indictment cites numerous acts taken by the conspirators to advance the plan, including purchasing supplies from a plumbing store and "maintaining a repository for bombs and bomb-making materials." Sounds a lot easier to prove than showing that Olson actually set the bomb, doesn't it?

But the 1976 trial never took place. Olson fled and evaded capture for twenty-three years, eventually making a life as a suburban homemaker in St. Paul, Minnesota, until she was arrested in 1999. She ultimately pled guilty to possessing explosives with the intent to murder and all other charges were dropped. She was sentenced to fourteen years in prison, although that sentence was subsequently reduced to thirteen years.

Conspiracy is another one of those controversial areas of criminal law. Defense attorneys regularly complain that prosecutors only charge conspiracy when they have weak evidence on the underlying crime. Sara Jane

Olson herself inveighed against conspiracy laws, saying that they are a threat to democracy and are unfairly used to target activists. Prosecutors counter that conspiracy law has always been a part of American law and that law enforcement needs this tool to target dangerous offenders like drug dealers, street gangs, and organized crime. They point out that the more people get together to plan a crime, the more likely the crime is to happen, and that conspiracy laws are needed to attack crimes in the planning stages.

CONSPIRACY THEORIES

Aside from criminal conspiracies, conspiracy theories have long been a part of our national culture. Some of the better-known conspiracies revolve around the September 11 attacks, the moon landing, the JFK assassination, and various theories about groups controlling the world. There are hundreds of books and web sites devoted both to perpetuating and debunking these theories.

Despite Olson's contentions that conspiracy is simply a tool for targeting activists, conspiracy is charged in many different types of cases. It has been used to help dismantle crime syndicates in major cities. The prosecutions following the largest business collapse in U.S. history were based on conspiracy charges. Enron's founder Kenneth Lay and former CEO Jeffrey Skilling were charged with conspiracy and fraud as prosecutors contend that they lied to investors about Enron's financial health. Even Michael Jackson's child molestation case included a conspiracy charge based on allegations that Jackson plotted to cover up his crimes by threatening witnesses if they accused him. Conspiracy is also frequently charged in cases involving terrorism, money laundering, drug distribution, stock manipulation, etc. In fact, part of the controversy surrounding conspiracy law is its popularity with prosecutors.

HISTORY LESSON

Conspiracy has a long tradition. The planned attack on Julius Caesar by Brutus and other plotters is perhaps one of the most famous and dramatized examples of group criminal activity:

O conspiracy
Sham'st thou to show thy dang'rous brow by night

> *When evils are most free? O then, by day*
> *Where wilt thou find a cavern dark enough*
> *To mask thy monstrous visage?*
>
> William Shakespeare, Brutus in Julius Caesar, act 2, scene 1

We all have a working knowledge of what a conspiracy might mean in everyday life (who hasn't suspected a conspiracy against them at work now and again?). But to appreciate the debate surrounding conspiracy, you need to understand exactly what conspiracy law entails and how powerful a tool it can be.

Like solicitation and attempt, conspiracy is a preliminary matter, meaning that it occurs before the contemplated crime. Conspiracy can have very serious consequences for two reasons:

1. those involved in a conspiracy can be convicted of *both* the conspiracy and the crime if it is carried out; and,
2. conspirators may be liable for crimes committed by other members of the conspiracy.

FANCY LEGAL TERM

You'll sound like a real lawyer if you refer to solicitation, attempt, and conspiracy as "inchoate" crimes. Actually, inchoate is not a legal term at all; it is just a word that means "in the early stages," which is what these three crimes are—the planning and action that precede the completion of the contemplated crime. Nevertheless, you are allowed to charge people $350 an hour to hear you talk like that.

The Agreement

The essential requirements of a conspiracy are:

1. an agreement between two or more people;
2. the intent to enter into the agreement; and
3. the intent to achieve the object of the agreement.

A conspiracy must involve a "meeting of the minds" between at least two people. No Abbott and Costello "who's on first" routines; each party has to understand the other, and they must be referring to a crime. And they must have a true criminal intent; if the conspiracy involves only two people, and one of them is an undercover police officer feigning participation in planning a major drug deal, no conspiracy has been formed.

WHARTON RULE

What is the rule regarding crimes that by their nature take two people to commit? Is a conspiracy always formed when contraband is sold? The basic rule is that there is no conspiracy unless more parties participate than are necessary to commit the crime. This is called the "Wharton Rule," named after its author Elizabeth Wharton (not really, although Elizabeth Wharton was an author and socialite, it was a different Wharton who wrote this rule in a legal commentary).

Each participant in a conspiracy must have actually intended to agree with someone else and each must also have intended to accomplish the objective of the conspiracy (the crime). The agreement doesn't have to be expressed formally; there is no need for the state to show a written contract to rob a bank (although that would be helpful to the DA). Nor does the agreement have to be verbal or even physical (a nod of the head). The agreement can be inferred from circumstances and the acts of the participants. Given the secretive nature of most criminal ventures, circumstantial evidence may be the only evidence available. Proof of cooperation between two people can substantiate a charge of conspiracy. With regard to proof of intent that the crime be accomplished, evidence that the defendant stood to gain financially or otherwise often suffices.

48 Hours: Mystery ran an episode called "Where Is Mrs. March," which told the story of a young wife and mother, Janet March, who vanished from Nashville, Tennessee, in August 1996. Her husband, Perry March, did not report her missing for two weeks and almost immediately became the prime suspect in her disappearance. However, he was not charged with her murder, and he moved with their children to Mexico to be near his father, Arthur March. Six years later the Nashville cold case squad took another look at Janet's disappearance and gathered enough evidence to indict Perry for murder. The Mexican authorities handed Perry over, and he was returned to Nashville to face trial.

Interesting, but what does this have to do with conspiracy, right? Ah, but that's the beauty of criminal law—there are always surprises, not least of which is how stupid some criminals can be.

While in jail on a $3 million bail, Perry apparently started thinking that his chances at trial might be a little bit better if Janet's parents, the Levines, didn't testify. Perry probably knew that Janet's mother would testify that

Janet was preparing to see a divorce lawyer right before her disappearance. Perry also knew that the Levines had long been convinced that their daughter had been murdered. So Perry made friends with fellow inmate Nate Farris. Perry told Farris that he could live the good life in Mexico (courtesy of Perry's father, Arthur) if he killed the Levines once he was released from prison.

Farris decided to use this circumstance to his advantage and went to the authorities. The police got him out of prison and had Farris secretly record phone conversations with both Perry and Arthur March about the proposed murders. Perry encouraged Farris and put him in contact with his father. Arthur March made plans with Farris to help him buy a gun and went to pick Farris up at the airport in Mexico two weeks later after Farris (falsely) told Arthur that the Levines had been killed. Both Perry and Arthur March were charged with conspiracy to commit murder. Arthur eventually entered into a plea bargain whereby he pled guilty to conspiracy and agreed to testify that Perry admitted killing Janet and that Arthur actually helped Perry dispose of Janet's body. (Perry was ultimately convicted of second-degree murder, among other charges, and sentenced to fifty-six years in prison.)

Multiple Crimes/Parties

Where there are multiple crimes over a period of time, the question is whether there is one conspiracy, or whether each crime is part of a separate conspiracy. The answer is found by looking to the original agreement. If two or more people agree to engage in *a course* of criminal activity, there is one conspiracy. In other words, if only a single agreement is made and that agreement happens to be to commit multiple crimes, there is still a single conspiracy. The thing to remember is that it is the *agreement* that constitutes the conspiracy, not the subsequent crime or crimes.

Another confusing situation arises when there are numerous people involved in the conspiracy (or conspiracies). Lawyers look at these complex enterprises in two ways. The first is called the "chain conspiracy." Here, there will typically be a series of agreements that are all part of a single, larger scheme. Each party to each agreement must intend the accomplishment of the overall criminal goal, and each participant is referred to as a "link" in the conspiracy "chain." Importantly, the prosecution is not required to prove that each participant specifically knew about the other participants (such as names, exact roles, etc.), as long as the participants knew that others must be involved and have the same interest in seeing the crime accomplished.

Chain conspiracies are typical of businesslike criminal enterprises, as with a large-scale drug operation. The "Snow Day" episode of *CSI: NY* (#71) offers a good example of such an operation. Drug Lord Gavin Wilder is trying to import nine hundred kilograms of cocaine into New York, and as the show opens, his men are busily hiding bundles of the drugs in big rigs that will eventually distribute the contraband around the city. However, their workday is interrupted when Detective Flack leads a raid on the distribution warehouse and seizes the cocaine (and also kills one of Wilder's men). After the wild shootout, Flack notes that Wilder has ties to every union in the city and would have no trouble moving all that cocaine (actually, *had* ties would be a more apt description, as the police eventually discover that Wilder had been shot in the back and killed, likely by one of his own men).

Obviously, Wilder's drug operation had several layers of workers. Some probably smuggled the drugs into the country, some others moved it to New York, and the men in the warehouse were packaging it so that truck drivers could deliver it around the city to union members and the like for final sale on the street. Each of these groups of workers had separate responsibilities and, very likely, they would not have had much contact with the other groups. The key point, though, is that each member of each group knew that he was involved in the illegal distribution of drugs, and it is this knowledge that links them all together in one conspiracy.

The second characterization of a complex conspiracy is called the "hub-and-spoke" arrangement. As the name suggests, when one person (the hub) enters into separate agreements with others (the spokes), and these persons are not involved in any way with the other agreements the hub makes, the individual agreements between the hub and each spoke are regarded as separate conspiracies. The only person involved in all of the separate conspiracies is the hub.

Overt Act

Although it used to be that the conspiracy was complete the moment the criminal agreement was reached, generally today courts also require that some "overt" act be done in furtherance of the conspiracy. The idea is to show that the conspiracy is more than just a shared wish and that the conspirators are actually "at work" trying to accomplish the criminal goal.

The "overt act" requirement is generally a fairly easy standard to meet. Basically, any action that has a tendency to further the object of the conspiracy will be sufficient. An "overt act" does not have to be a substantial step toward completing the crime; even simple preparatory acts count.

Returning to our Sara Jane Olson example, just buying readily available products at a plumbing supply store was an overt act in the conspiracy to commit murder—even before they were assembled into an explosive device.

What wouldn't count, though, are conversations among the parties in reaching the agreement since this is merely part of the agreement. But pretty much anything else that tends to show that the conspirators meant to carry out the crime meets the standard. And remember, this is a group activity, so as soon as *any one* of the participants commits an act in further-ance of the conspiracy, all members become liable for the conspiracy.

WHEN DOES IT END?

For some purposes (for example, statute of limitations questions), it is important to determine when a conspiracy ends. The main issue is usually whether acts designed to conceal the crime are part of the conspiracy itself (and thus stop the statute of limitations from run-ning). The general rule is that unless the concealment was part of the conspiracy agreement, any acts taken to avoid detection are not part of the conspiracy. The reasoning is that all criminals try to conceal their crimes, and unless there is evidence that the coconspirators somehow planned to hide their criminal acts, the conspiracy is not continued by virtue of their acting like every other criminal.

Defenses

There are defenses to conspiracy, the first of which is "withdrawal." What if at some time prior to the bomb going off and killing a police officer, Sara Jane Olson had withdrawn from the conspiracy to plant the bomb? Not guilty? Not quite. Although it sounds like it might be fair to let Olson off the hook because she either realized the error of her ways or was at least frightened enough about being caught to stop participating, her with-drawal would probably not be an effective defense.

Remember, a conspiracy is complete once there is an agreement and an overt act in furtherance of the conspiracy. That's it; game over. A more modern view, expressed in the Model Penal Code, is that Olson could avoid liability by *thwarting the success of the conspiracy* (by informing the police who then actually prevent the crime) and by a *complete and volun-tary renunciation of the conspiracy.*

In episode #31 of *Without a Trace* called "Trip Box," three firefighter bud-dies agree to burn a building down in exchange for a loan stark canceling the large gambling debt of one of them. At a backyard barbecue, Gus, the gambling firefighter, convinces Billy and Scott to help him "just this once." The conspiracy is formed the minute they all reluctantly agree to the plan. The "overt act" requirement is met when one of them obtains a "trip box," a device used to make a fire look like as if it had been caused by faulty wiring.

On the day of the planned fire, Scott says that he can't go through with it. He *asks Gus not to do it*, but does nothing to stop the plan (by going to the police, etc.). In fact, Scott actually helps the conspiracy succeed by rescuing the other two from the fire and taking the "trip box" from the scene of the crime. Thus, there is little likelihood that Scott could escape liability for the conspiracy despite his disavowal. Not that it would matter much, since later in the episode he is killed by the loan shark who made the initial deal with Gus.

Most courts agree that "impossibility" is not a defense to conspiracy. The conspirators cannot escape punishment by arguing that they would not have been able to accomplish their criminal objective.

Special Problems

There are some issues peculiar to conspiracy law. For example, what if someone is charged with conspiracy, but all the other alleged conspirators have previously been acquitted in separate trials? Generally speaking, this defendant could *not* be convicted of conspiracy since there is logically no one he could have agreed with. This differs from the situation where other conspirators are not apprehended; in that case, the defendant may still be convicted of conspiracy if there is evidence that she entered into an agreement with at least one other person to commit a crime (even if that person is still at large).

Liability for Crimes of Coconspirators

A powerful and far-reaching principle of conspiracy is that each participant is liable for all crimes committed by all other members that were:

1. reasonably foreseeable as a result of the conspiracy, and
2. committed in furtherance of the conspiracy.

Let's say you enter into a conspiracy to rob a bank. You provide some key information about the bank's security, but you're out of the country when the bank is robbed. You could still be held liable for larceny if a coconspirator stole a car to use as a getaway vehicle as well as assault if a coconspirator assaulted a security guard at the bank.

You wouldn't be liable for *all* crimes committed by the coconspirators. If during the robbery one of the coconspirators sexually assaulted a person in the bank, you would not be charged with that crime since it was not a reasonably foreseeable part of the robbery and was not committed to further the robbery.

Think about it; you can be liable for crimes of your coconspirators, even if you took no part in these other crimes, even if you had no knowledge whatsoever about them. The rule is under attack in some states and may be limited in others, but it would be wise for any potential conspirator to remember the saying: in for a penny, in for a pound—or twenty to life.

One limitation on this rule involves *withdrawing from the conspiracy*. While simply withdrawing is generally *not* a defense to the conspiracy charge itself, it *can* prevent liability for other crimes committed by the coconspirators. To be effective the withdrawal must go well beyond saying "I quit" silently to yourself. The conspirator must communicate this renunciation to other members of the conspiracy in such a manner and time that they would also have time to reconsider their participation. If there is an effective withdrawal, the conspirator will still be liable for the conspiracy (unless she goes further and thwarts the objective of the conspiracy), but will not be liable for crimes committed by other members of the conspiracy.

Advantages for Prosecution

The reasoning behind conspiracy law is that it allows the government to step in at a stage before the criminal objective has been accomplished. The law also recognizes that two people united to commit a crime are likely more dangerous than either one alone. But, it's not hard to see why prosecutors are especially fond of conspiracy law.

Conspiracy law allows prosecutors to increase punishment by charging someone with not only the substantive crime, but also with conspiracy and even other crimes committed by coconspirators. Conspiracy law also enables the prosecution to get into evidence at trial some things that otherwise would be inadmissible. For example, statements of conspirators are admissible against coconspirators (whereas they might be inadmissible hearsay otherwise). Finally, prosecutors have enormous flexibility in deciding what conduct of the defendant they will use as proof of her guilt;

they can focus on statements and actions of the defendant where they have strong evidence and ignore areas where their evidence is weak.

Critics of conspiracy law note that it has historically been used to prosecute controversial activities by workers and activists. They also point out that because it emphasizes "thought" more than "acts," there is an increased danger that people will be prosecuted for what they say and who they associate with, which undercuts basic principles of our justice system. Despite its controversial nature, conspiracy law is alive and well and being used in courtrooms (and television dramas) across the country.

Legal Briefs

Conspiracy—an agreement between two or more persons to commit a crime.

Inchoate crimes—planning or early-stage crimes; solicitation, attempt, conspiracy.

Wharton rule—no conspiracy unless more parties participate than are necessary to commit the crime.

Chain conspiracy—a series of agreements that are all part of a single plan.

Hub-and-spoke conspiracy—one person (the hub) enters into *separate* agreements with others.

Overt act—almost any action that shows the conspirators were taking steps to complete the crime.

Withdrawal—traditionally not a defense; modern view is that it *can* be a defense where the defendant thwarts the success of the conspiracy (by informing the police) and completely and voluntarily renounces the conspiracy.

Chapter 16 ⚖

Attempt

It is every parent's worst nightmare—a grown man using the Internet to seduce a child. We all know how easy it is to hide your identity on the Internet; what happens when some pervert starts chatting with an impressionable twelve or thirteen-year-old online? It all probably seems safe to the child—but nothing could be further from the truth.

Sadly, there are adults out there who troll the Internet, looking for the right victim. Once they find him or her, they'll spend hours, days, weeks even, chatting, joking, finally building to what it is they are really after—a meeting to engage in sexual activity. Maybe the adult starts hinting about getting together, sending pictures of himself, asking about the child's sexual experiences and preferences. Once the child lets slip that mom and dad will be gone for the night, the predator leaps at the chance. He suggests they get together to show how much they "care" about one another. And once he arrives . . .

If there's any justice in the world, he'll meet NBC correspondent Chris Hansen working on another episode of *Dateline NBC: To Catch a Predator*, and he'll be arrested and prosecuted. Starting in 2004, *Dateline* has produced a series of investigative shows looking into what it calls a national epidemic of men using the Internet to look for sex with children. The show used online decoys provided by the group Perverted Justice to make the men think they were meeting children when in fact they were coming to a house (in locations across the country) where they would be filmed meeting with Hansen (and after some shows, immediately arrested).

These men were all attempting crimes related to molesting children. Obviously the ones in the *Dateline* investigations didn't succeed, but they surely demonstrated blameworthiness and dangerousness to society. This is exactly what the crime of attempt addresses.

RIPPED FROM THE *DATELINE*

Law & Order did a show in 2006 ("Public Service Homicide," #376) about a tabloid television show called *Hard Focus* that used decoys from a group called "ScumWatch" to identify online pedophile predators and lure them to a location where they would be filmed and interviewed (sound familiar?). When a man, Carl Mullaly, is murdered within hours of being outed on the nationally televised *Hard Focus*, Detectives Martin and Govich are on the case.

In true *Law & Order* tradition, the case is more complicated than a vigilante killing a pedophile. It turns out that a producer from *Hard Focus* was also trying to build interest in a show called *Confront and Heal*, in which people who had been molested as children confronted their abusers. This producer, Ellie Harper, arranged for one of Mullaly's previous victims to meet with him. Harper, knowing this victim wanted to kill Mullaly, actually gave her a knife and a camera to take to the meeting. At the show's conclusion, Harper was convicted of "depraved indifference" murder for, as McCoy said, "putting two trains directly on a collision course."

Usually when someone tries and falls short of the mark, we encourage them to give it another shot; after all, that's just good manners. Not so in criminal law. We make it a crime to *attempt to commit* a felony or misdemeanor. (Which is somewhat mean-spirited—the person's self-esteem is already shaken because he didn't get the job done, and now you're telling him he's not just a loser, he's a criminal.)

A criminal attempt is an act done with the intention of committing a crime that for some reason does not result in completing the crime. Criminal law doesn't punish people for thoughts, so an attempted crime must be based on more than the *intent* to commit a crime or some statement about wanting to commit a crime; there must also be a *sufficient step toward* the attempted crime. This fits with our basic definition of a crime as having both a mental state (here the specific intent to commit the attempted crime) and a physical act (here the step toward committing that crime).

Mental State

Although this is a bit tricky, attempt actually requires two intents: (1) the intent to do the act that results in the attempt; and (2) the *specific* intent to commit the crime attempted.

Suppose your neighbor isn't home and you decide to take his riding mower to cut your grass with the intention of returning it as soon as you're done. As you're entering his garage, he pulls into the driveway and calls the police. Have you committed attempted larceny? No. You certainly intended to walk over there and take the mower, but you lacked the *specific intent* to permanently deprive your neighbor of his property (the requirement for larceny), so you did *not* attempt a larceny.

Let's use the infamous case of Claus von Bulow to illustrate the dual intents necessary to prove an attempt. In this well-known tale of familial bliss, American heiress and socialite Sunny Crawford married Claus von Bulow in 1966. By 1980 there was serious tension in their marriage. On December 21, 1980, Sunny and family were celebrating Christmas at the family mansion in Newport, Rhode Island, when she mysteriously became ill and lapsed into a coma. The coma was attributed to hypoglycemia from an insulin injection. Claus argued in favor of turning off life-support means, but surprisingly Sunny continued to breathe on her own (although she remained in a persistent vegetative state).

The authorities investigated the circumstances surrounding Sunny's coma and presented evidence to a grand jury. The grand jury apparently found enough motive (the terms of Sunny and Claus's prenuptial agreement said that he would get nothing if they divorced, but $14 million if he was a widower) and physical evidence (a black bag with drugs and a syringe with traces of insulin in it) to indict Claus on charges of attempted murder. The prosecution's theory was that Claus von Bulow intentionally gave Sunny an injection because he specifically wanted her dead so that he could inherit a fortune.

This case meets the dual intent criteria for an attempt. Claus *meant* to give Sunny the insulin injection, and he specifically *meant* to murder her. Claus was convicted after a very public trial, but the conviction was overturned on appeal (leading to an excellent performance by Jeremy Irons as Claus von Bulow in the movie *Reversal of Fortune*).

Sufficient Step

In order to show that the defendant was actually trying to accomplish the criminal activity, the state needs to prove some sufficient act or step toward committing the crime. The obvious question is what constitutes a sufficient act; in other words, how close does the defendant have to come to committing the crime to call it an attempt? Courts have struggled with this issue, coming up with a variety of "tests" to answer the question.

Tests have focused on what remains to be done before the crime can be completed—has the defendant gone far enough in preparing for the crime that the only thing left is to actually commit the crime? Other analyses ask what the defendant has *already* done and try to determine whether the defendant would have ceased efforts to commit the crime but for some intervening cause.

The Model Penal Code approach is more specific. It requires a "substantial step" toward committing the crime that shows "strong corroboration" of criminal purpose. The MPC also has a list of acts that the jury can consider (if, of course, the prosecution proves they happened), among which are:

1. lying in wait or following the intended victim
2. enticing the intended victim to a particular place where the crime will happen
3. unlawfully entering the place where the crime is to happen
4. possessing or making materials to be used in the crime.

These (and other acts like these) are the basis upon which a jury could find that the defendant took a sufficient step toward the commission of the crime to find him guilty of attempt.

One important point to make is that no matter the test used (a particular state's or the MPC's), the act required for an attempt is more substantial than the "overt act" required for a conspiracy. A conspiracy only requires an act that can actually be a fairly minor step toward completing the conspiracy, while an attempt requires an act that moves significantly toward the intended crime. An act that might suffice to prove a conspiracy might not be substantial enough to prove an attempt.

BY THE NUMBERS

We are a nation that believes in striving to attain goals. As with anything else, we have many people trying to commit crimes. According to the *Criminal Victimization in the United States, 2005 Statistical Tables*, in 2005, there were over 3 million attempted crimes of violence, over 180,000 attempted robberies, and over 480,000 attempted thefts (Table 59).

Defenses

An attempt is, by definition, a crime that didn't happen. What if the crime couldn't have happened; what if it had been *impossible* for the crime to be completed? Is that a defense to a charge of attempt? Leave it to lawyers to make such distinctions, but the general rule is that "legal impossibility" is a defense to attempt, but that "factual impossibility" is a *not* a defense.

"Legal impossibility" arises when a person has a misunderstanding of the law. Say that you try to enter a state park at night believing that the park is closed to the public after dusk, but for some reason you don't make it (your car breaks down). In fact, the park is open twenty-four hours a day. You are not guilty of attempting to trespass since your mistaken belief as to the law does not create any criminal liability. You have not actually shown any willingness to do anything contrary to public safety, and you're not much of a threat.

For an example of factual impossibility, let's look back at *Dateline: To Catch a Predator*. In each of the instances shown (and there were dozens of them), the man came to the home thinking that the person with whom he been chatting was a child. The fact that the person the defendant was talking to was actually an adult made the crime of child molestation a factual impossibility.

While none of these men could have committed the crimes they intended, each clearly demonstrated his dangerousness to society and the fact that he was willing to act in a manner meant to commit a crime (some of these men drove for hours to get to the meeting places; many also brought alcohol and condoms). The law simply won't allow these men to escape punishment just because the facts weren't exactly how they believed them to be.

What about a withdrawal? If the defendant has done some act that is a substantial step toward completing the crime, may she escape punishment by abandoning her plan? The traditional answer was "no"; once the defendant demonstrates her dangerousness by taking a substantial step toward the crime, the attempt has already taken place.

The Model Penal Code and modern statutes do allow a defense of abandonment provided:

1. the abandonment is entirely voluntary (i.e., not motivated by an unexpected circumstance like an increased likelihood of being caught); and

2. the abandonment is complete and not simply a postponement to a more opportune time.

Punishment

The Model Penal Code authorizes the same punishment for an attempt as for the completed crime. Some states impose half the punishment that would be imposed for the completed crime. In the event that the crime is completed, the attempt is said to "merge" with the completed crime, and a defendant cannot be convicted of both an attempt and the completed crime.

Legal Briefs

Attempt—an act done with the intention of completing a crime that for some reason does not result in completing the crime; the defendant must have both the intent to do the act that results in the attempt and the specific intent to commit the crime attempted.

Sufficient step—Under the Model Penal Code it is a substantial step toward committing the crime, which shows strong corroboration of criminal purpose; other courts look at whether the defendant has gone far enough that the only thing left is committing the crime; still other courts look at what the defendant has already done to determine whether she would have ceased efforts to commit the crime save for some intervening cause.

Legal impossibility—a valid defense to attempt involving a misunderstanding of the law such that the "attempt" does not violate any law.

Factual impossibility—not a defense to attempt; where the defendant acts to cause a result that would be a crime, but because of things he does not know it is not possible to commit the crime.

Chapter 17   ⚖️

Accomplice Liability

It seems like every time the police are on a manhunt (person hunt?) on a TV show, they eventually burst into someone's apartment, summarize the person's connection to the sought-after criminal, and proceed to squeeze information out of the initially tough-talking sap by threatening to lock him up as an "accessory" or an "accomplice." The sap almost instantly caves because, hey, who wants be convicted when they really didn't do anything but give a little aid and comfort to an ex friend/lover/cellmate/ pen pal?

It sounds like a pretty good threat. The police officers on the shows make it seem that a person is an accomplice if he did anything at all to help the "perp" in any way. But, while accomplice liability is a fairly broad concept, it's not quite as elastic as it can sound on TV.

The Basics

People participate in criminal offenses in varying ways and to varying degrees. One person might be on the lookout for tipsy patrons leaving a bar, and his partner-in-crime might be the one to hold the gun and say "Put 'em up!" The person who actually commits a crime (in this case, robbery) is referred to as the principal, and anyone who assists him in perpetrating the crime is an accomplice.

Responsibility for a crime is not limited to the person who actually commits the offense. We also believe in punishing those who encourage the defendant to commit the crime, those who assist in perpetrating the crime, and those who interfere with the apprehension of the offender.

Traditional Concepts

In the old days, the parties to a crime were meticulously classified. The person who actually committed the crime was the "principal in the first degree." Others involved in the crime were called the "principal in the second degree," "accessory before the fact," "accessory after the fact," or "accessories for that cute little black dress." If convicted, these people were guilty of the *same offense* as the perpetrator of the crime (the principal in the first degree) and subject to the same punishment.

Conspirator vs. Accomplice

Unlike accomplices who assist or encourage the commission of a crime, conspirators are those who have made *an agreement* to commit a crime, and they are considered principals of the crime of conspiracy. Of course, they cannot be convicted of conspiracy until an "overt act" toward perpetrating the crime has been made by at least one of them.

In this era of very formal pleadings, it was vitally important that the prosecution properly classify those involved in the crime; if a person was charged as an "accessory before the fact" and the evidence showed that she was an "accessory after the fact," she could not be convicted. This type of formalism proved to be needlessly confusing.

Modern Statutes

One major change is that a person who provides assistance after a crime (what used to be called an "accessory after the fact") doesn't face the same punishment as the principal. Those who provide assistance *after* the crime are usually guilty of a separate offense that generally carries a lower penalty.

To be found guilty of this crime (sometime called "harboring a fugitive" or "obstructing justice"), the defendant must have assisted someone who completed a *felony*, and the defendant must have *known* that the person committed a felony. The assistance must have been given directly to the felon with the intent of impeding the police.

Basically, if you knowingly help someone evade capture or prosecution, you can be charged. For example, Seth Jeffs, younger brother of polygamist Warren Jeffs (the leader of the Fundamentalist Church of Jesus Christ of Latter-Day Saints who was charged with arranging a marriage between a sixteen-year-old girl and a married man and fleeing prosecution), was arrested in October 2005 and charged with "concealing a fugitive." When he was stopped for a traffic violation, Seth Jeffs had $142,000 in cash, $7,000 in prepaid debit and cell phone cards, and his brother's personal records. Although Warren Jeffs was not physically "concealed" in the car Seth Jeffs was driving, it was pretty clear that Seth was helping his brother stay on the lam. (The Warren Jeffs case was followed throughout 2006 on shows such as *America's Most Wanted* and *Larry King Live* and appears to have been the inspiration for 2007 episode of *Numb3rs* called "Nine Wives.")

The infamous beating death of Matthew Shepard in Wyoming involved a failed attempt to obstruct justice when Shepard's murderer, Aaron McKinney, asked friends to help him hide his involvement in the crime. Chastity Pasley, the girlfriend of McKinney's codefendant Russell Henderson, testified that she and others tried to provide the defendants with alibis, disposed of Henderson's bloody clothes, and hid his bloody shoes in a storage shed. Pasley pled guilty to being an "accessory after the fact" (the term is still in use in some jurisdictions). Obviously, Pasley knew that a crime had been committed and that McKinney and Henderson had committed it. But she was sentenced to 15-to-24 months in prison, much less than the punishment given to those who perpetrated this heinous crime.

Requirements for Accomplice Liability

In 1995, Texas teenager Adrianne Jones was discovered in a field in Grand Prairie, Texas, shot twice in the head. Her murder went unsolved for nearly nine months. Then Diane Zamora, a freshman at the Naval Academy in Annapolis, confessed to her roommates that she had killed someone. The roommates reported this shocking news to the naval chaplain, and the police soon arrested both Zamora and her fiancé, David Graham.

The subsequent investigation revealed that while Zamora and Graham were apparently a perfectly happy, loving high-school couple, Graham at one point told Zamora that he had had a sexual encounter with Jones, a fellow student on the track team. (there is some dispute as to whether this actually happened or if Graham concocted the story to make Zamora jealous). According to prosecutors, Zamora was so jealous that she demanded Graham atone for his actions by killing Jones.

Graham and Zamora carried out their plan. Graham asked Jones out and drove to a deserted area. Zamora, secreted in the backseat, grabbed Jones and hit her in the head with a weight, but Jones managed to escape the car. Graham then tracked her down and shot her in the head. They disposed of their clothes and went home. Although Graham actually shot and killed Jones, was Zamora any less responsible?

The basic requirements of accomplice liability are that the person aided or abetted the criminal act, that she did so with the necessary intent, and that the crime was completed. Aiding or abetting means that the person encouraged the commission of the crime. Essentially, any *significant assistance* meets the standard. Acts like distracting potential witnesses or providing helpful information certainly can count, as would driving the getaway car for a bank robber. The assistance does *not* have to be critical or essential to committing the crime; even if it can be shown that the crime would have been committed without the accomplice's assistance, the accomplice may still be convicted.

Do You Have to Be the Police?

In most cases, failing to prevent the commission of a crime will *not* be considered aiding or abetting, although there may be some rare instances where a person has a legal obligation to intervene and where the failure to do so will be seen as an act that aided the commission of a crime.

In the Jones case (which received great national attention and was made into an NBC movie, *Love's Deadly Triangle: The Texas Cadet Murder*), Zamora clearly aided and abetted the murder. Her assistance included both planning and initiating the attack.

It is also a crime to incite or encourage a felony even if no practical, physical assistance is given. Of course, the criminal has to be aware of the encouragement; else it could hardly be encouraging, could it? Just being present at the crime scene probably is not enough to be considered inciting the crime, unless there is a prior agreement that the person will help in the commission of the crime if necessary. That is just the kind of confidence-giving measure that would likely encourage someone to commit a crime.

Zamora plainly incited Graham to kill Jones. In his confession, Graham said that Zamora actually demanded Jones's death to satisfy her need for vengeance; Zamora apparently made it clear to Graham that the only way to prove his love for her was to kill her rival. In fact, it could be argued that simply by agreeing to be in the car, Zamora gave encouragement to Graham.

Mental State

The mental state required for accomplice liability is twofold. First, the accomplice must have the state of mind necessary to commit the crime herself; in other words, the accomplice must have the same state of mind as the principal. In our example, Zamora clearly intended Jones's death every bit as much as Graham did.

Second, the prosecution must show that the accomplice's assistance or encouragement was given with the affirmative desire that her actions would have the assisting or encouraging effect. It is not enough to show that the defendant simply *knew* that her conduct would facilitate the crime. Zamora obviously meets this second mental state requirement as well.

WHAT IF THE PERPETRATOR ISN'T CONVICTED?

Although the crime must actually have been committed, it is *not* necessary for the perpetrator to be convicted in order to convict the accomplice (the perpetrator escapes, dies, etc.). As long as the prosecution proves the perpetrator's guilt, the accomplice may be found guilty.

Scope of Liability

The basic rule is that the accomplice is liable not only for the crime she aided or incited, but also for all reasonably foreseeable crimes that result from the intended crime. If you are the lookout for a bank robbery during the course of which a security guard is killed, you can be found guilty as an accomplice not only of the robbery but also of the murder (which was a reasonably foreseeable result of an armed bank robbery). Some courts limit liability to what crimes you *actually* anticipated, not those that you should have considered.

Defense

An effective withdrawal from the crime *is* a defense to accomplice liability. The withdrawal must occur prior to the commission of the crime or the time when stopping the crime would be impossible. Where actual physical assistance was given (aiding and abetting), the withdrawal must include taking action to render the assistance ineffective (where you provided a gun for a robbery, taking the gun back). Where only encouragement was given (inciting), the withdrawal can be accomplished by a renunciation of the encouragement. Of course, this renunciation can't just be a thought in your head; you must communicate it to the perpetrator.

Legal Briefs

Principal—the person who actually commits a crime.

Accomplice—a person who aids or abets the commission of a crime.

Requirements for accomplice liability—must provide substantial assistance to the principal; must have the mental state necessary for the crime and must have intended that her actions would have an encouraging effect on the principal.

Scope of liability—basic rule is that the accomplice is liable not only for the crime she aided, but also for all reasonably foreseeable crimes that result.

Defense to accomplice liability—withdrawal is a defense; must be prior to commission of the crime and include rendering assistance given ineffective or renouncing encouragement.

Chapter 18 ⚖

Justification

Under certain conditions, conduct that would otherwise be criminal is viewed by society as *justified* and is not punished. Sometimes society says that normally "bad" conduct is acceptable and even to be encouraged. We usually do not promote punching someone in the face, but we look at it differently if the person smacked was an armed robber and the "attacker" was a passerby foiling the robber's escape. Defenses to criminal liability based on these principles are, not surprisingly, known as "justification defenses." Justification defenses include self-defense, defense-of-others, defense-of-property, and necessity, among others.

If it is blazingly clear that the conduct was justified, there might not be an arrest or trial at all. On the other hand, sometimes a trial is the best way to sort things out. If there is a trial, it is up to the defendant to raise at least some evidence of justification as a defense.

Self-Defense

In a first season episode of *Shark* called "Sins of the Mother," the police are called to the apartment of low-life drug dealer Jeremy Clinton, who has been killed by two gunshots to the chest. On the scene, the police find married socialite Sarah Metcalfe. She claims to have been carrying on an affair with Clinton (now where have I heard that before?) and says that when she came over to break it off, Clinton attacked her, leaving her with no choice but to shoot him with his own gun in self-defense.

The law of self-defense says that a person charged with an assault crime (simple assault all the way up to murder) can claim self-defense if she *used the amount of force that reasonably seemed necessary to protect herself from the imminent use of unlawful force on her.*

The defendant must *reasonably believe* that it was necessary to defend herself. Remember, anytime you see "reasonable" in criminal law, it relates to an objective standard; the issue is not simply what this particular defendant believed was necessary, but whether this was a belief that a reasonable person would have held.

As always, the question of exactly "who" is the reasonable person is a tricky one. Consider the infamous self-defense claim of "subway vigilante" Bernhard Goetz. On December 22, 1984, Goetz entered a subway car at the Fourteenth Street station in New York City. Soon after he took his seat, four young African-American men approached Goetz and asked him for money. Goetz, who had previously been the victim of a mugging, pulled a gun from his jacket and fired five times. Although all four young men survived, one was permanently paralyzed. At his trial, Goetz claimed that a reasonable person would have felt threatened because the youth's actions were the beginning of an armed robbery.

In assessing Goetz's actions, should the "reasonable person" be an experienced subway rider who may have seen robberies on the train or even someone who has been the victim of a mugging before? Should the "reasonable person" be someone who feels threatened enough to carry a gun in the first place? The risk of course, is that the more the "reasonable person" is imbued with Goetz's characteristics, the less objective the standard. On the other hand, a person who has been subjected to past violence may reasonably react in a different manner than someone who has not. Not surprisingly, states vary on how much subjectivity can be included in the reasonable person standard.

In addition, the defendant must reasonably believe that the threatened harm was *unlawful*. If a police officer uses force to make a lawful arrest (grabs the defendant, places handcuffs on, etc.), the defendant is not entitled to claim self-defense when he resists arrest and knees the officer in the groin.

UNLAWFUL ARRESTS

What if the arrest is unlawful? In most states, if the defendant knows that the arresting person is a police officer, she may not use force to resist arrest. That's because the legality of an arrest can be a complex question best resolved later by legal processes. Obviously there is a burden with an unlawful arrest (who wants to be booked and held overnight?), but the potential cost of a struggle with an armed officer is extremely high. Nevertheless, in cases where the officer uses excessive force to make an arrest, it may be acceptable for the defendant to use force to resist.

Importantly, the threat must have been of *physical harm*—the fact that a romantic rival threatened your relationship by flirting with your boyfriend wouldn't legally justify you hitting her with a barstool. And the threat of physical harm must have been *imminent*. This means that the person threatening the defendant must have appeared both willing and able to harm the defendant. The person asserting self-defense isn't required to wait until the attacker actually lunges with the knife, but self-defense would have to be based on more than the fact that the alleged attacker stood up from his seat with a mean look on his face. In assessing whether the threat of physical harm was imminent, all the circumstances surrounding the incident, including threatening language, presence of weapons, and physical movements may be considered. There are no hard-and-fast rules here; common sense and a basic understanding of human nature decide the issue.

Going back to our *Shark* episode, it appears that Sarah Metcalfe met the requirements for using self-defense. Clinton's assault on her was plainly unlawful since all she did was tell him the affair was over. He threatened actual physical harm, threatening to kill her, and it seems likely that Sarah could reasonably believe that she needed to use force to protect herself.

But Sebastian Stark sees a way to blow Sarah's claim of self-defense out of the water. He focuses on the fact that Clinton was shot twice; in his view, the first shot would clearly have disabled Clinton and the second shot was plainly because Sarah Metcalfe wanted Clinton dead. So while the first shot may have been in self-defense, the second shot was not necessary to protect Sarah from any physical harm—the second shot was murder, not self-defense.

Deadly Force

There is a rule of *proportionality* that applies to self-defense. Just as it sounds, the defender cannot use force that is excessive with regard to the threatened harm. A person may use nondeadly force against a nondeadly threat or even a deadly threat. But a person is *not* justified in using deadly force against a nondeadly threat. Again, this is common sense; the law simply won't condone a shooting death in response to a rude push after a fender-bender. The bottom line: deadly force may only be used in situations where the defendant reasonably believed that the person was about to inflict death or serious bodily injury on her.

DEADLY FORCE

Despite its name, the use of deadly force does not have to result in a death. It is usually defined as force that was *intended to cause death or serious bodily injury* (not a black eye, but probably a serious concussion) or which created the *substantial risk of death or serious bodily injury* (swinging a tire iron at someone's head, shooting at someone, etc.). Even if the defendant claims that he shot at the attacker simply to scare him or at most "wing" him, shooting at a person obviously creates a very real risk of death or serious injury and will almost always be considered use of deadly force.

Consider the Minnesota case where a hunter shot and killed six deer hunters and wounded two others. The defendant, Chai Soua Vang, was hunting when he got lost and went into a tree stand on private property. Terry Willers arrived and asked Vang to leave. Other hunters, companions of Willers', arrived and also asked Vang to leave, threatening to report him to the game warden for trespassing.

Vang claimed that he acted in self-defense when he opened fire because one of the hunters angrily shouted racial slurs at him while another fired a shot at Vang. The surviving hunters testified that no one in the group fired until Vang had already started shooting. Crucially, during the trial, Vang said that one of the hunters deserved to die because he had given Vang "the finger" and called him names. The jury rejected Vang's claim of self-defense, apparently believing that Vang used deadly force in response to the use of racial slurs and angry words.

In addition, simply because someone tries to use deadly force does not automatically allow the defendant to use deadly force in response. The deadly force used in self-defense must have been *necessary*. If the defendant realizes that nondeadly force will protect her, she is required to use only that level of force.

Duty to Retreat

The general rule is that there is no duty to retreat before using nondeadly force in self-defense, even if retreating could be done safely and at no further risk to either party. When rap singer Foxy Brown kicked an employee of a nail salon and smacked a second worker in the face during an argument over payment, either worker might have been able to flee to a secure spot in the store, but they were not required to and would have been justified in using force to repel Brown's attack.

A more difficult question arises with respect to the use of deadly force. Is a defendant justified in using deadly force if he had an opportunity to safely retreat? Some states require the defendant to show that he had no opportunity to retreat before using deadly force. The underlying principle is that human life should only be jeopardized where absolutely necessary.

Even in states that require retreat, there are significant limitations on the duty. Retreat is commonly only called for where it can be done in *complete* safety. More than likely, a person wouldn't have time to calmly and quietly consider the possible alternatives to using a rock to bash the head of the mugger holding a knife; the test is what the defendant *reasonably believed* about retreat possibly increasing the risk of injury to himself.

Usually retreat is not required if the defendant is attacked in her own home. The home is a person's "castle" and is itself a sanctuary from violence; to demand retreat from this haven would be unreasonable. In episode #92 of *Without a Trace*, Agent Malone and company are looking for the Jordano family, who are reported missing after a relative goes to their home and finds a broken front door and blood all over the living room. As usual, they were gone "without a trace" (unless you count the blood and signs of a struggle).

It turns out that the blood was not from the family at all. Rather, the father, Ted Jordano, shot and killed a hit man who broke into the family home at night carrying a gun with a silencer. The hit man was after Ted's son Dylan, who happened to witness a member of an Albanian gang kill a man in an alley. Based on the information Ted had from his son, Ted armed himself and waited for the attacker. Maybe it would have been smarter for Ted to call the police, but the law would probably not require him to retreat from his own home. In fact, Ted would probably not even have faced any charges (he eventually agreed to have his son testify against the gang in exchange for placement in the witness protection program). Who could find fault with a father protecting his home and young son from a killer?

COHABITATION

What about domestic violence? In states that require retreat, is there a duty to retreat if the attacker has the same right to be in the "castle"? The general rule is that the attacker's right to be in the home is irrelevant, and the defendant has no duty to retreat before using deadly force.

In some states there is no duty to retreat at all, even if the defendant could have done so in complete safety. The reasoning is that a person should have the right to defend herself against an attack and shouldn't be required to "give in" to an attacker. Nevertheless, the fact that retreat could have been made in complete safety *can* be considered in determining whether the use of deadly force was "reasonably necessary."

It's not clear in the TV world of *Shark* whether there is a duty to retreat. Obviously if there were, Stark's case against Sarah Metcalfe would appear to be stronger because he could argue that Sarah could have retreated in complete safety while holding the gun after having already shot and disabled Clinton.

Right of Aggressor to Self-Defense

The simple rule is that the aggressor in a physical attack cannot claim self-defense in using force to defend himself from the victim. By starting the conflict, the aggressor forfeits his right to self-defense (the victim of his attack may lawfully use force to defend herself, and a person can only use self-defense to resist *unlawful* attacks).

However, the right to self-defense is unlike virginity in that you *can* regain it. If the aggressor uses nondeadly force and the victim responds with deadly force, the initial aggressor is entitled to use whatever force is reasonably necessary to stop the counterattack (recall that a victim's use of deadly force in response to a nondeadly attack is *unlawful*). Also, the aggressor may regain her right to self-defense if she *withdraws* from the confrontation. This commonly means actually leaving the scene of the attack or at least communicating the intent to withdraw to the victim. Of course, if you've already assaulted someone, it may be a difficult task to convince your victim that you intend to stop. But something very definitive, like actually leaving or laying down your weapon, will likely suffice.

Battered Victim Claiming Self-Defense

According to prosecutors, California homemaker Susan Polk considered several options for killing her husband Felix: drowning, running him over in a car, or using a shotgun. She eventually settled on using a knife. The couple's fifteen-year-old son discovered his father's body lying face up in a pool of blood in the guest cottage at the family's California home.

Although Susan initially denied killing her husband, she subsequently admitted stabbing Felix after he lunged at her with a knife. She claimed that it was self-defense after years of physical and emotional abuse during their thirty-year marriage.

By any measure, the Polk's marriage had an unusual beginning. Felix was Susan's therapist when she was just a teenager, but soon become her lover. They were married when Susan was twenty-five and had a marriage that was dysfunctional in many ways. In fact, they were in the process of getting divorced when Felix was killed. Prosecutors theorized that Susan was distraught because a judge had granted custody of the Polks' son to Felix and had given Felix the family home. According to the prosecution, Susan was dangerously angry when she went to see Felix at the family home that night.

Susan Polk defended herself at the trial. One of her sons testified against her while another son testified on her behalf, saying that he had also suffered emotional and physical abuse at the hands of his father.

SECOND CHANCES

As if Susan Polk's trial weren't unusual enough (with her examining and cross-examining her own sons), there was another twist that brought even more attention to this case. Polk's first trial ended in a mistrial when the wife of her attorney was brutally murdered. A teenage neighbor was arrested and charged with that unrelated murder. Polk defended herself in her second trial.

Self-defense is often an issue in cases where the defendant (usually a woman, but not always) relies on a long history of mental and/or physical abuse to justify using force (often deadly) against her abuser.

A particular problem arises when the defendant attacks the abuser during a time when no abuse is actually occurring. Typically the defendant might say that she killed her abuser at an opportune time because he was threatening to harm her again in the future and/or had made specific threats about killing her if she tried to leave or go to the authorities. The obvious problem is that this harm is not "imminent" as is required by the law of self-defense.

Some courts will allow expert testimony on "battered woman syndrome," which suggests that the battering history led the defendant to believe that the only way to prevent further violence was to kill or disable her abuser. While this type of testimony actually addresses the question of whether the force used by the defendant was "reasonably necessary," the defendant can also argue that with no way to leave the relationship and further violence a certainty, the harm was inevitable if not imminent.

Defense of Others

Generally, a person (the "hero") is justified in using force to protect someone else (a third party) from an unlawful use of force by an aggressor (the "bad guy"). Essentially, the hero who intervenes on behalf of the third party places herself "in the shoes" of the third party and can use force to the extent that the third party would be justified in using force (i.e., where the bad guy's use of force is unlawful).

In 2006, Mary Winkler was accused of killing her preacher husband with a shotgun in their home in Tennessee. In his opening statement, her lawyer said that Mary was actually trying to protect the couple's one-year-old daughter from her abusive husband when the shotgun she was pointing at him accidentally went off. The defense also argued that Mary had suffered years of physical and sexual abuse at the hands of her husband. The prosecution contended that Mary was actually trying to hide a check-kiting scheme from her husband and that she killed him before they were scheduled to meet with their local bank. Mary Winkler was convicted of voluntary manslaughter, and in May 2007 she was sentenced to three years in prison.

In our *Shark* episode, it turns out that the bad person, Clinton, was actually shot twice by different guns. Sarah's husband Richard explains that he was the second shooter. He suspected that Sarah was having an affair and followed her to Clinton's apartment. When he got there, he witnessed Sarah and Clinton struggling over a gun. The gun discharged, hitting Clinton. Nevertheless, Clinton continued to come after Sarah and Richard had no choice but to defend Sarah's life by shooting Clinton. It seems like that scenario could be defense-of-others (we later discover that Sarah and Richard's daughter Jordan, who was actually fathered by Clinton back when Sarah was a drug-using prostitute, shot Clinton and that it was Sarah who shot Clinton the second time, although it was Jordan's shot that actually killed Clinton—it all made sense in the show).

Can you claim defense of others when you don't specifically know who it is you are defending? You can try. Imagine a scenario where a crusader kills a madman who might have gone on to kill hundreds or even thousands of innocent people if he were not stopped. Surely that must qualify as defense of others, right? Not according to the jury in episode #144 of *Law & Order: SVU*.

In that episode, AIDS prevention activist Gabriel Thomason brutally murdered two gay men who were drug addicts and carriers of a new and untreatable strain of HIV and who both continued to have unprotected sex with multiple partners. Thomason's own brother was infected by one of the murder victims. Thomason freely confessed to the murders, but argued that he did it in defense of the other hundreds of men who could ultimately have been infected with the new strain of HIV. In fact, in the closing argument, Thomason's attorney compared Thomason's situation to one where Osama bin Laden is prepared to detonate a "dirty" bomb in Manhattan unless he is killed.

Apparently the jury felt that the danger to others was not sufficiently imminent to support a defense-of-others claim, and Thomason was convicted on two counts of second-degree murder. (Interestingly, the father of one of Thomason's victims said in his victim-impact statement at sentencing that while he did not approve of Thomason's actions, he could understand and asked that the judge not punish Thomason too severely. The judge gave Thomason the minimum sentence.)

An issue sometimes arises when the hero defends the third party in a situation where the third party did *not* have the right to self-defense (the "bad guy" is actually an undercover police officer making a lawful arrest). Some courts will not allow a claim of defense-of-others in this case (because they don't want to encourage people to get involved in altercations unless they know the facts), while others will allow it as long as it *reasonably* appeared that the third party was actually entitled to use force in self-defense.

Defense of a Dwelling

If our houses are our castles, we should be able to kill any knave who tries to breach our walls, right? In the "good old days" you could use deadly force to prevent someone from even entering your home (provided you at least warned the person to stop). Not anymore.

Generally, modern statutes allow the use of deadly force only when the defendant reasonably believes the intruder intends to commit a felony or harm someone in the dwelling. Sometimes the use of deadly force is limited to cases where the defendant reasonably believed the intruder intended to commit a felony (so, if it was clear that the defendant was going to hit the defendant—a *misdemeanor* simple assault—the defendant could not lawfully shoot and kill the intruder).

YOUR "STUFF"

No surprises here. You can use nondeadly force to protect your possessions, but you are not allowed to use deadly force. Essentially, we value human life over your stuff. So no stabbing the guy who picked your pocket, no shooting the gal running out of your house with your brand-new Rolex.

Making Arrests

Making an arrest can sometimes require the use of force (except in L.A., where it seems that the police are required to beat the snot out of the suspect). The basic rule is that a police officer can use nondeadly force to arrest anyone she reasonably believes has committed a misdemeanor or a felony and can use deadly force where she believes the person has committed a felony. As long as the officer reasonably believed the person arrested had committed the crime, the use of force is justified even if the arrested person is later found to be innocent.

The modern trend, however, has been to limit the use of deadly force to *dangerous* felonies (kidnapping, rape, murder, burglary, etc.). The rationale is that the defendant has already shown by his conduct that he is a danger to society, and greater force, even deadly force, may be used to protect us all.

In cases where the officer is met with violence in trying to make the arrest, she may use force in her defense, perhaps even deadly force. However, this situation would actually be controlled by the laws of self-defense.

Legal Briefs

Justification—situations where normally criminal behavior is accepted, even encouraged.

Self-defense—the right to use the amount of force reasonably necessary to protect oneself from the imminent use of illegal force.

Deadly force—force that was intended to cause death or serious bodily injury or which creates a substantial risk of death or serious bodily injury; does not have to result in death.

Duty to retreat—generally there is no duty to retreat before using nondeadly force in self-defense; some states allow deadly force only where there was no safe avenue of retreat.

Regaining the right to self-defense—aggressor can regain right to self-defense where she withdraws from the confrontation or where she was using nondeadly force and the victim responds with deadly force.

Defense of others—a person who intervenes on behalf of a third party places himself in the shoes of the third party and can use force to the extent the third party could.

Defense of dwelling—can use deadly force only where the defendant reasonably believed the intruder intended to commit a felony or harm someone in the dwelling.

Chapter 19   ⚖️

Necessity and Duress

There are other justification defenses aside from self-defense, defense-of-others, etc. Sometimes a defendant claims that although she committed a crime, she had no other choice. These types of defenses ask the justice system to look beyond the immediate criminal conduct and consider the broader picture. In the defendant's view, if we do this, we will see that her actions should not be punished.

Necessity

Necessity may be the mother of invention, but it is also sometimes the mother of crime. A person who has been accused of a crime may make a claim of necessity ("I had to do it") if he can show that committing the crime prevented a greater harm. Usually this defense works when the defendant faced the choice of committing a relatively minor offense or allowing himself or others to suffer a great harm (exceeding the speed limit in order to get a seriously injured child to the emergency room).

Necessity is closely related to the defense of duress. The major distinction between the two is that necessity applies when the pressure to commit the crime is created by the environment or physical forces of nature. If another *person* is exerting the pressure, the proper defense would be duress.

EXCUSE VS. JUSTIFICATION

In criminal law there are subtle differences between defenses based on justification and defenses based on excuse. One of the differences is that "justification" means that society actually encourages the defendant's conduct under the circumstances, while "excuse" means that even though the defendant has harmed society in some way, she should not be blamed for the harm. Necessity is a justification defense and duress is an excuse defense, although the distinction is often ignored.

In order to mount a successful necessity, the defendant must show that the threatened harm was imminent; if it wasn't, there would likely have been options other than committing a crime to avoid the harm. Society would prefer that you not commit a crime unless there is no time to take a less drastic course.

Imagine your car breaks down on a country road on a sunny spring day. Do you have a valid necessity defense if you break into a nearby unoccupied farmhouse after waiting an hour for someone to drive by and offer assistance? Probably not. The answer might be different if it was a bitterly cold night winter night and you were about to suffer frostbite. What if there were a legal alternative available? In our "wintry" disabled car scenario, what if you had just passed an open restaurant a few hundred yards down the road but you just didn't feel like walking to it? You wouldn't be able to claim necessity for breaking into the home.

Generally, you can only claim necessity if you chose the *least harmful* alternative available. This is a commonsense balancing test. If you really were risking frostbite on a little-traveled country road, you might have a successful necessity defense if you broke into a house, but not if you decided to set the house on fire to make yourself toasty warm. Also, the harm caused by violating the law must be less serious than the harm sought to be avoided. Again, this is a commonsense judgment.

Although necessity is often an issue where the defendant has committed a relatively minor offense (speeding, trespassing), it is sometimes raised in more serious cases. Recall the murder trial of anti-abortion activist James Kopp. In 1988, Kopp slipped into the woods behind the home of Dr. Barnett Slepian, an upstate New York obstetrician who provided abortion services. Kopp fired a high-powered rifle and killed Slepian, who was with family members in the kitchen. Kopp fled the woods and embarked on a three-and-a-half-year flight from justice that ultimately ended when he was extradited from France.

Part of Kopp's defense was that he acted out of necessity. In his view he was obliged to stop the systematic murder of unborn children, and the only means available to him at the time was to shoot abortion providers like Slepian (Kopp said that he actually only intended to wound Slepian and that the bullet took a "crazy ricochet" after hitting Slepian in the shoulder). Essentially, Kopp's argument was that he committed a crime to prevent a greater evil.

Although it seems like this is a duress defense, since Slepian is a person, Kopp was not saying that Slepian himself put pressure on Kopp to shoot, but rather that the broader society or environment that allows abortions made him do it. And therein was the problem with Kopp's necessity argument. Abortions were legal in New York, and the "evil" that he sought to prevent was not one recognized by society—so it was not possible to justify the crime Kopp committed. In 2003, Kopp was sentenced to twenty-five years to life for the murder of Slepian.

BREAK OUT

Escaped convicts sometimes rely on a necessity defense after their capture. They argue that escape was justified since they did it to avoid a greater harm, such as assaults in prison. To be successful, they would have to show that there were no reasonable, legal alternatives (such as informing authorities). They would probably also have to show that they voluntarily surrendered once they escaped the prison and immediate danger. They rarely do, and their necessity defenses rarely succeed.

Duress

Legal duress occurs when a threat is made to use violence against the defendant (or another) unless the defendant commits a crime. The threats made by the other person must be of some immediate, serious physical harm to the defendant or some other person (perhaps even a stranger to the defendant). Of course, the defendant must be aware of the threat and must have a reasonable belief that the threat is sufficiently serious to be coercive (it won't work if the defendant says that he robbed the store because a bully threatened to give him a "wedgie" if he didn't).

As with necessity, the defendant must show that he had no opportunity to avoid the harm by some legal alternative (going to the police, etc.). And in no case is duress a defense to intentional murder; society is never going to say that taking a life is the lesser of two harms (although the defendant could introduce evidence of coercion to negate an element of a murder charge, such as premeditation).

A plausible scenario for a duress defense was portrayed in the "Money for Nothing" episode of *CSI: Miami* (#41). The show opened with an armored car on its way to the Federal Reserve Bank being attacked and robbed in the streets of Miami. Coincidentally, Horatio was nearby and he heroically tried to foil the machine gun attack by shooting one of the robbers with his pistol. The remaining robber escaped with $3.2 million, but the supremely effective CSI detectives used their high-tech wizardry to capture him shortly thereafter in a swamp. Much to their surprise, they found that the money they recovered was counterfeit.

Horatio and the CSI team eventually discover that the security guards transporting the money switched the real currency for the fake stuff just before the unrelated armed robbery. It turns out that the previous night one of the security guards, Paul Donlon, received a phone call in which he found out that his younger sister, Mary, had been kidnapped. The kidnappers demanded that Paul make the switch. The only words he heard his sister say were, "Do what they say or they'll kill me!"

This is exactly the sort of threat that makes for a duress defense; in these circumstances, a reasonable person might believe the threat would be carried out and feel compelled to avoid that outcome by doing something illegal. The question would be whether Paul had a reasonable alternative to committing the larceny. Could he have called the police or at least alerted the armored car company? (We later find out that Mary was in on the kidnap plan and intended to flee the country with the money—poor guy, used by his sister and arrested by Horatio.) Paul is marched out of the CSI offices in handcuffs, and Horatio assures Paul he'll be fine in prison. Better advice to Paul would have been to get a good lawyer and argue duress.

Legal Briefs

Necessity—a justification defense where the defendant argues that he committed the crime to avoid an imminent threat of harm from his surroundings.

Duress—an excuse defense where the defendant argues that he committed the crime to avoid an imminent threat of physical harm from another.

Chapter 20 ——————————— ⚖

Entrapment

From the time we are children we are told that creativity is a good thing and that we should engage in inventive thinking whenever we can. However, criminal law is one place where creativity can be problematic. For instance, when the intent to commit a crime originates not with the defendant, but rather from the ingenuity of the police, we call it entrapment and don't punish the defendant.

In "The Wrath of Khan" episode of *Shark*, Stark and his minions go after Amir Khan, a billionaire import-export businessman who also happens to be an international arms smuggler (isn't that always the way?). Khan has been selling explosives and "surplus Taliban" weapons to L.A. gangs, and the explosives he sold have been traced to three recent car-bombings and nine deaths. The only problem is that the FBI wants him, too (although as we later find out, not to prosecute Khan but to protect him as a valuable spy).

To prevent the feds from snatching Khan, Stark hurriedly tries to finish a six-month police investigation into Khan, which has included placing a confidential informant in Khan's employ. Stark wants Khan to make one more sale of C-4 explosives to undercover officers so they can arrest and prosecute him. While the team outlines the plan to the two undercover agents, DDAs Casey Woodland and Raina Trey say that although the defense will "argue entrapment," they don't have time to pull back if Khan gets suspicious, so they have to push Khan into making the sale.

There are two elements to an entrapment defense:

1. The criminal intent must have *originated* with law enforcement; and

2. The defendant must not have been predisposed to commit the crime prior to coming into contact with law enforcement.

There are two basic ways courts assess entrapment defenses. The traditional way is to look *subjectively* at the defendant's actions and determine whether police inducements or the defendant's own predisposition caused the defendant to commit the crime. Importantly, the simple fact that the police presented the defendant with the opportunity to commit the crime is *not* in itself entrapment (it is not entrapment if an undercover officer buys drugs or stolen property).

The key issue is the defendant's predisposition; if the evidence shows that she was predisposed to commit the crime (had previously committed related offenses, jumped at the opportunity, etc.), the level of police inducement is irrelevant. However, where there is little or no evidence of predisposition and it can be shown that the police had sufficient contact with the defendant prior to the crime (repeated entreaties, providing means and information helpful to committing the crime, etc.), entrapment may be a valid defense.

In our *Shark* episode, it sure sounds like entrapment when the DA's office encourages the police to really "push" Khan into selling the illegal explosives. On the other hand, the six-month investigation that produced evidence that Khan had previously sold arms to L.A. gangs surely seems to show that the criminal intent did not originate with the police and that Khan was very much predisposed to commit the crime. It seems that any level of inducement used by the undercover officers short of putting a gun to Khan's head would still not support an entrapment defense.

The other test that courts sometimes apply is an *objective* test that focuses exclusively on the police officer's actions and ignores the defendant's subjective state of mind. Under this approach, the focus is not on whether the "innocent" defendant was induced to commit the crime, but rather whether the police overstepped their bounds. The question is whether the police conduct was such as was likely to cause an innocent person (not *this* defendant) to commit the crime. If it appears that the average person with no predisposition to commit the crime would have been impelled to act by the police, the defendant has been entrapped. The defendant's own predisposition is not relevant.

There are two important limitations on this defense, no matter which test is used. The first is that entrapment is generally not applicable to serious crimes like murder or rape or even serious assaults. The principle is that no matter from where the intent to commit these dangerous crimes arose, the defendant is to be held responsible for violating social norms.

The second limitation on the defense is that only the police and their agents can "entrap." A defendant cannot argue that a private citizen entrapped her *unless* the private citizen is actually working for the police (for example, an informant who is paid by the police). It wouldn't be sporting to allow the police to skirt the rules on entrapment by relying on proxies.

Legal Briefs

Entrapment—defense where the criminal intent originated with law enforcement and the defendant was not predisposed to commit the crime prior to contact with law enforcement.

Subjective test—looks at the defendant's actions to determine whether law enforcement inducements or the defendant's own predisposition caused the defendant to commit the crime.

Objective test—focuses exclusively on the actions of law enforcement to see if their actions would have caused an innocent person (not *this* defendant) to commit the crime.

Chapter 21 ⚖️

Intoxication

Like college students, defendants will often try to avoid responsibility for their actions by claiming that they were too drunk or high to know what they were doing. For better or worse, drug and alcohol intoxication is common in our society, and since impaired thinking often leads to bad decisions, it's no surprise that alcohol and drugs frequently play a role in criminal activity. It's also no surprise that criminal law has devised rules to handle these claims. Although intoxication usually involves alcohol or drugs, the rules apply even to prescription medicine and the like.

DRUG AND ALCOHOL USE

According to *Criminal Victimization in the United States, 2005 Statistical Tables*, in 27.5 percent of all crimes of violence in 2005 (not including murder) the offender was perceived to be under the influence of drugs or alcohol. The true number could be much higher since in over 49 percent of the cases the victim was unsure whether the offender was intoxicated (Table 32).

There is an important legal distinction between *voluntary* and *involuntary* intoxication.

Voluntary Intoxication

The traditional rule was that voluntary intoxication was irrelevant to criminal liability. If you went out and got roaring drunk and assaulted a police officer, robbed a store, or stole a wallet, you weren't able to claim that Jim Beam made you do it (unless you have an actual friend named Jim Beam who coerced you, in which case you might have a duress defense). That's still the case today. As with college guys caught cheating on their girlfriends, being voluntarily drunk or high is not a defense to any crime.

Nevertheless, many states *will* allow evidence of voluntary intoxication to negate the mental state required for certain crimes (technically, this isn't a "defense" since what the defendant is really doing is challenging whether the prosecution has proved the elements of its case). Generally, courts only allow voluntary intoxication to negate the *specific intent* required to commit crimes (like assault with the intent to murder, which requires the specific intent to kill). A defendant could offer proof that his intoxication left him without the ability to form a specific intent to kill.

Where the crime is a general intent crime (simple assault), voluntary intoxication cannot negate the general intent requirement and has no bearing on criminal liability. The same goes for strict liability crimes (statutory rape) where voluntary intoxication is likewise irrelevant.

Involuntary Intoxication

How many times has a co-ed with a hangover been scolded by a significant other or parent with these words: "Did someone put a gun to your head and *make* you drink eighteen Jell-O shots last night?" While the answer is generally a sheepish "no" followed by a plea to close the shades and stop shouting, that's precisely the situation where the criminal law would give you a break.

The basic rule is that involuntary intoxication *is* a defense to liability if it rendered the person insane under the insanity test applied in that state. Intoxication is involuntary if the defendant did not know the substance was intoxicating or he consumed it under duress (someone held a gun to him and ordered him to take the drugs).

There is a question as to whether a permanent impairment to the brain caused by repeated *voluntary* intoxications (a lifelong drinking problem) can be the basis for an insanity defense. Some states would probably allow the defense; others would not.

Legal Briefs

Voluntary intoxication—generally *not* a defense; in some situations can be used to negate the mental state required for a crime.

Involuntary intoxication—where the defendant did not know the substance was intoxicating or consumed it under duress; generally a defense, particularly where the intoxication rendered the defendant insane under the applicable state test.

Chapter 22 ⚖

Insanity

Some crimes are susceptible to ready explanation: an addict wants money for her next score, so she lifts a twenty from her roommate's purse; a jealous husband attacks his romantic rival with a tire iron. Maybe it's not what we would do (or at least not what we imagine we would do), but there's nothing about these crimes that falls outside our general understanding of human behavior. That's not the case with all the crimes we read about and see on TV. Some criminal cases are so bizarre or monstrous that they defy understanding and make us ask: "Was that [guy/lady] completely *nuts*?"

On June 20, 2001, Andrea Yates killed her five young children (Noah, age 7; John age 5; Paul, age 3; Luke, age 2; Mary, age 6 months) by drowning them in the bathtub. She then called 911 and was arrested. She had a history of postpartum depression and was under the care of a psychiatrist at the time of the killings. In March 2001, just months before the murders and while her fifth child was still an infant, Yates became severely depressed following the death of her father and was admitted to a hospital and treated. A new doctor recommended a change in Andrea's medications that occurred just days before the murders.

Yates asserted postpartum psychosis as the reason for the killings. In March 2002, a jury rejected that defense and found her guilty. She was sentenced to life in prison with eligibility for parole in forty years. That verdict was later overturned and, at her retrial, Yates was found not guilty by reason of insanity and was committed to a state mental hospital.

RIPPED FROM THE SCRIPT?

The verdict from Yates's first trial was overturned based on a strange twist in the *Law & Order* blueprint of basing shows on real-life crimes. During the first trial a psychiatrist gave testimony that shortly before the killings, an episode of *Law & Order* had shown a woman who drowned her children and had been acquitted by reason of insanity. In fact, no such episode existed. The appellate court found that the jury might have been influenced by the testimony and ordered the new trial. Of course, not missing a trick, *Law & Order: Criminal Intent* later did an episode based on the Yates case ("Magnificat," #73).

Let's get some things out of the way right up front. Yes, many folks who commit crimes probably have some form of mental illness (diagnosed or undiagnosed). And, yes, perhaps the fact that a person commits a crime is itself an indicator of mental abnormality (most "normal" people would find choose a different course of action). But that's not within the purview of criminal law.

Legally, insanity means that the defendant is entitled to an acquittal (usually by a finding of "not guilty by reason of insanity," or NGRI) if at the time of the crime he was so impaired by mental illness as to be insane within the meaning of the law. In federal court and in most states, a person acquitted by reason of insanity is automatically committed to a hospital for some period of time. Usually the defendant will be held until he can prove that he is no longer a danger to society. It is important to remember that insanity is *a legal term*, not a psychiatric one, and that there may be significant differences between the two.

COMPETENCY

Insanity is a question of the defendant's state of mind *at the time of the crime*. Competency to stand trial is an entirely separate question of the defendant's state of mind *at the time of the trial*. A defendant is incompetent to stand trial if she does not have sufficient ability to consult with her lawyers with a reasonable degree of rationality (basically if she can't participate in her own defense) or if she does not have a sufficient factual understanding of the judicial proceedings (if she can't understand what the trial is for and what the possible consequences are). A finding that the defendant is not competent is *not* a defense to the charges, but will result in a postponement of the trial until the defendant is found competent (if ever).

Insanity is a catchall term that encompasses many possible mental abnormalities that have only one thing in common—they can result in an acquittal of criminal charges. The exact cause of a defendant's mental illness is usually not relevant. Andrea Yates's lawyers presented evidence that they felt showed not only that she was insane when she committed the murders, but also what caused it. But whether her insanity was caused by the death of her father, postpartum depression, a change in medications, or her having been abducted by space aliens, the only relevant finding the second jury made was that she met the legal definition of insanity. In many states mental retardation can render a person legally insane (if the person satisfies the criteria of insanity).

PSYCHOPATHS

What about a person who manifests a mental abnormality by repeatedly committing crimes despite punishment, imprisonment, attempts at rehabilitation, etc.? Should this person be entitled to an acquittal because he's "insane"? (Why else continue on this irrational path?) The short answer is "no." In many states an "antisocial personality" exhibited by continual criminal conduct is not legal insanity. Bottom line—you aren't entitled to an insanity acquittal just because you commit lots of crimes.

Tests for Insanity

There are two basic ways to meet the definition of insanity in criminal law:

1. a *cognitive impairment* that affects the defendant's ability to understand reality and think about it rationally; and
2. a *volitional impairment* that interferes with the defendant's ability to control her actions, even though she may know that what she is doing is wrong.

Various "tests" have been proposed that are based on one or both of these factors, but since the workings of the human mind are understood imperfectly at best and the insanity defense has historically been such a polarizing social issue, many states have had difficulty settling on one "test" or another.

The M'Naghten Rule

The traditional standard for insanity was set forth in England and adopted here by most states. The *M'Naghten* rule is a *cognitive test* only (a defendant's inability to control her actions [volition] is irrelevant), so it is considered more restrictive than other insanity tests. Under the *M'Naghten* rule, a defendant is entitled to an acquittal if because of her mental impairment she lacked the ability at the time of her actions to either:

1. know the wrongfulness of her actions; or
2. understand the nature of her actions.

Obviously there is a lot of room for interpretation under this test (a common criticism of all insanity tests). Courts have developed clarifications for what it takes to meet this test; perhaps predictably, they often differ from state to state. Nevertheless, certain key points are generally accepted.

If a defendant does not understand the actual real-world, physical consequences of his action (he does not realize that a blow from a hammer can injure a human skull), he probably meets the *M'Naghten* test (he doesn't understand the nature of his actions). Take the 2005 case of Charles McCoy Jr., the Ohio man charged with shooting at two homes, a school, a car dealership, and eight moving cars over a period of four months, killing one person and causing widespread fear in central Ohio. His defense was that because of severe paranoid schizophrenia and his refusal to take medications, he did not appreciate the wrongfulness of his actions when he seemingly randomly opened fire over those four months (he eventually dropped his insanity defense and agreed to serve twenty-seven years in prison).

What about a person who is suffering from delusions (false beliefs)? Is that person entitled to an acquittal under the *M'Naghten* rule? For example, what if McCoy had asserted that he was delusional and he thought the people in the school, car dealership, cars, etc. were actually planning to kill him. Under the *M'Naghten* rule, the question would be whether if things had been as McCoy believed he would have been entitled to take the actions he took. Here, the answer would be "no"; his belief that others were planning to kill him did not give him the legal right to shoot them.

Suppose someone believes that her actions are morally right even if she knows that they are criminal. For example, a woman who because of some mental impairment honestly believes that it is proper for her to kill her cheating spouse. In most states she would not be entitled to a finding of not guilty by reason of insanity, since her impairment only led to her subjective belief that killing was acceptable (and she understood that it was "wrong" in society's view).

Loss of Control Test

The basic criticism of the *M'Naghten* test is that it does not apply to those mentally impaired persons who are simply unable to control their actions.

In the eyes of some, the fact that a person is unable to control her conduct does not make her morally culpable and deserving of punishment.

Some states have (or had) tests that include the *M'Naghten* test and further provide that a person is insane if she has a mental impairment so that she lacks the capacity to conform her conduct to the requirements of the law. This is sometimes referred to as the "irresistible impulse" test in that it applies to those who have some impulse that overcomes their will to avoid what they know to be wrong. And despite the terms "loss of control" and "irresistible impulse," the incitement to commit the crime does not have to hit the defendant suddenly or without warning.

Critics of "loss of control" tests contend that only in exceptionally rare cases would a person truly be unable to stop herself from doing something that she knows is wrong. Further, they say it is impossible for any jury to know whether a defendant was unable to control herself at a particular time and that jurors are simply left to flip a coin between conflicting expert (psychiatric) testimony. Of course, this last criticism (about dueling experts) could be made about any insanity test.

The Durham Test

A third test that goes beyond either the *M'Naghten* or loss of control tests is the *Durham* test, after the case of that name, once used in New Hampshire and Washington, D.C. This test requires an acquittal if the crime was the *product of an impairment* that the defendant had when he committed the crime. This very broad test seems to give little direction to a jury, and many argue that it would simply be too confusing to apply.

FOR THE LOVE OF JODIE FOSTER . . .

One of the most famous examples of a successful insanity defense is that of John Hinckley Jr., who attempted to assassinate President Reagan on March 30, 1981. Hinckley claims to have watched the movie *Taxi Driver* repeatedly (in which a disturbed man plans to assassinate the president) and developed an obsession with actress Jodie Foster. Hinckley's assassination attempt was apparently an effort to gain Foster's attention. He undoubtedly did, although not in a good way. Hinckley was found not guilty by reason of insanity and committed to a psychiatric hospital in Washington, D.C.

As things stand, the law on insanity is an area that is continually evolving. Some courts would expand the "test" for insanity and allow an acquittal where the jury feels that a defendant's actions were caused by a mental impairment such that he is not morally responsible for his conduct. On the other hand, some courts would further restrict the defense and follow a modified *M'Naghten* test that allows an acquittal only if the defendant was incapable of knowing the nature and quality of his action *and* of knowing right from wrong. Several states have simply abolished the insanity defense altogether. Others have added another possible verdict to "guilty," "not guilty," and "not guilty by reason of insanity"—"guilty but mentally ill." A verdict of "guilty but mentally ill" holds the defendant criminally liable for her crime, but recognizes that mental illness played a role in the crime and allows that state to treat the defendant while incarcerated.

This is obviously a sensitive and emotional topic since it goes to the very heart of what criminal law is about—punishing those who are morally responsible for bad conduct. In that regard, the back-and-forth debates about just when a person cannot be held responsible is to be expected. What we probably cannot expect anytime soon is an answer that will settle the debate.

Legal Briefs

Insanity—a legal, not psychiatric, term that encompasses many possible mental abnormalities that can result in an acquittal.

Competency—the defendant's state of mind at the time of the trial; a defendant is incompetent if she cannot participate in her defense or understand the nature of the charges against her.

Cognitive impairment—an interference with a person's ability to understand and think about reality.

Volitional impairment—an interference with a person's ability to control her actions.

M'Naghten **rule**—the traditional test for insanity asks whether the defendant lacked the ability to (1) know the wrongfulness of his actions; or (2) understand the nature of his actions.

Loss of control test—provides that a person is insane if she has a mental impairment such that she lacks the capacity to conform her conduct to the requirements of the law.

Durham **test**—requires an acquittal if the crime was the product of an impairment that the defendant had when he committed the crime; perhaps the broadest of the insanity tests.

Chapter 23 —————————   ⚖

The Exclusionary Rule

The exclusionary rule sounds like a holdover from elementary school recess, where the popular kids decided who played in the games and who sat on the sidelines. But nothing arouses anger around the watercooler more than a dirty, low-life thug going free because some moronic, criminal-loving judge ruled that clear evidence of guilt couldn't be used at trial. "Dammit, we're not safe enough as it is; how can the court let this dirtbag escape responsibility *when we all know he did it!*"

The only way excluding evidence of guilt makes sense is to realize that a criminal trial is not only about seeking justice in this particular case, it's also about upholding fairness in the criminal justice system as a whole.

A judge is obviously aware that if she excludes evidence of guilt, a defendant might go unpunished, but the judge has a responsibility to ensure the integrity of the entire system, and allowing the prosecution to use illegally obtained evidence taints not only this trial but our system of criminal law. No one likes it when an apparently guilty person goes free, but this is a *product* of the exclusionary rule, not its aim. The focus of the exclusionary rule is squarely on discouraging police misbehavior.

The exclusionary rule was adopted by the U.S. Supreme Court and applies in both federal and state courts. The rule *prohibits evidence obtained in violation of the defendant's constitutional rights from being used at trial to prove guilt*. The purpose of this judge-made rule is to dissuade the police from violating a defendant's constitutional rights; after all, if the evidence cannot be used at trial to prove guilt, it's useless to the police, so the idea is that the police won't waste their time with illegal searches and seizures. If they do anyway, their efforts will go for naught since the evidence won't be admissible at trial to get a conviction.

OPTIONS

Excluding evidence from trial is not the only way to punish police misconduct. The consequence for an illegal search could be administrative in nature—perhaps departmental discipline or even a hearing before an independent panel of citizens. The penalties could run from fines to suspensions and terminations. We could also rely on civil suits where those wronged pursue damages against the responsible officers in civil court. Despite these options, our system continues to rely on the exclusionary rule as the most direct and appropriate approach to police misconduct in obtaining evidence.

Illegally obtained evidence can encompass all types of physical evidence. When Robert Blake was charged with murdering his wife, he sought to suppress some fifty pieces of evidence taken from his home, including firearms, ammunition, documents, telephone records, cash, and even the videotape of the search itself. He argued that when the police allowed author Miles Corwin (doing research on a book) to be present during the search, they violated his constitutional rights (the Supreme Court has said it is a violation of the Fourth Amendment for third parties unrelated to the execution of the warrant to be present at searches). Blake sought the suppression of all fifty pieces of evidence.

The judge's ruling in the Blake suppression hearing highlights an important aspect of the exclusionary rule—it is *not* automatically applied in all cases where there has been an improper (unconstitutional) search. Where the link between the police misconduct and the evidence obtained is weak or attenuated, a court may not see much use in excluding the evidence. Remember, although criminal law is filled with definitions and rules, it also allows for common sense (sometimes).

That's what happened in the Blake case. Superior Court Judge Schempp (please fill in your own *Three Stooges* joke) ruled that there was a clear Fourth Amendment violation when the officers invited Corwin to come. However, she also found that since Corwin didn't recover any evidence and remembered few details about the search of Blake's home, she would not exclude the fifty pieces of evidence.

General Scope

The general rule is that not only must the illegally obtained evidence be excluded, but also *any evidence obtained as a result of the illegally obtained evidence.* Courts refer to this additional evidence as tainted "fruit of the poisonous tree" and will exclude it from trial.

Nevertheless, the additional evidence may be admissible at trial as to guilt under certain circumstances. The two major ways in which the prosecution can have illegally obtained evidence admitted are:

independent source: Evidence will be admissible at trial if the prosecution can show that it was obtained in a way that is not connected to the illegal search or seizure. Perhaps some officers barged into a warehouse without a warrant on a simple hunch while at the same time detectives were working with an informant who provided them with reliable information that would have allowed the detectives to get a warrant to search the warehouse.

inevitable discovery: If the prosecution can show that the police would have inevitably discovered the additional evidence regardless of their illegal conduct, the additional evidence may be admissible.

In the *Law & Order* episode "Thinking Makes It So" (#367), Detectives Fontana and Green finally corner one of the kidnappers of a six-year-old girl at the home of the kidnapper's ex-wife. Fontana threatens to kill the man (and also dunks his head in a toilet) in an effort to make the kidnapper reveal the location of the girl—which he does. The girl was hidden on the ex-wife's yacht in the nearby harbor. The defense eventually argues to a judge that the coerced confession led to the girl being found and that the kidnapping charge should be dismissed because of the "fruit of the poisonous tree" doctrine.

ADA Borgia uses "inevitable discovery" to save the day. Her interview of the ex-wife (who was actually at the house when the detectives arrived) revealed that the ex-wife was aware that her former husband had just recently been on the yacht. Borgia argues that Fontana would surely have interviewed the ex-wife, who would have told him this information and that Fontana would inevitably have searched the yacht and found the girl. The judge agrees with Borgia, and the defendant was convicted of both robbery and kidnapping.

WHERE THE RULE DOESN'T APPLY

Generally the exclusionary rule does not apply outside of the criminal trial itself. The Supreme Court is aware of the high cost of allowing potentially guilty persons to go unpunished and has been reluctant to extend the reach of the exclusionary rule. So evidence obtained by an illegal search or seizure is usually admissible during grand jury proceedings, bail hearings, and sentencing hearings.

Enforcing the Rule

In our system, a judge does not on his own initiative review the evidence to be used at trial; any issues as to illegally obtained evidence must be raised by the defendant. Once raised, the defendant gets a hearing about the evidence in front of the Judge (usually called a "suppression hearing," since the defense is asking the judge to suppress or keep out the evidence). The judge listens to testimony, hears arguments, and then decides whether the evidence was illegally obtained and, if so, exactly what evidence is excluded.

In many cases key parts of the story about the allegedly illegally obtained evidence will need to come from the defendant (did he give police permission to search his apartment?), but a defendant might be reluctant to testify for fear of implicating himself in the crime. To address this concern, the Supreme Court has said that a defendant's testimony at a suppression hearing may *not* be used against him at trial. The idea is to allow the judge to hear both sides of the story and come to a fair resolution of the issue.

Although it is the defendant's responsibility to raise the issue of illegally obtained evidence, the burden at the suppression hearing is on the government. It is up to the prosecution to prove that the evidence should not be excluded. The prosecution does not have to prove the evidence was properly obtained "beyond a reasonable doubt," but only by the lower standard of "preponderance of the evidence."

Exceptions to the Rule

As all lawyers know, the only absolute rule in criminal law is that there are exceptions to every rule. If you feel the urge to argue about that statement, you are already thinking like a lawyer (bonus points if you felt the urge to hold a press conference).

Anyway, the Supreme Court has designated a few areas where it feels that excluding evidence would not do much to deter improper police activity. In other words, illegally obtained evidence is not necessarily kept out of the trial. The major exceptions are:

Impeachment Exception

While illegally obtained evidence cannot be used by the prosecution to prove its case, the evidence may be used to *impeach* the defendant if he testifies. Courts aren't keen on perjury, and if the defendant is going to take the stand and lie, the prosecution can challenge his credibility even with improperly obtained evidence. Of course, the jury will be told that the illegally obtained evidence can only be used in judging the defendant's veracity and not as evidence of the crime he's charged with (good luck with that).

IMPEACHMENT

Impeachment is a nice lawyerly was of challenging the veracity of a statement. It is basically a way of calling someone a liar. This is not the same thing as charging a political official with malfeasance in office, although there will undoubtedly be some accusations of lying made there also (perhaps not very politely).

Private Party Exception

The Fourth Amendment only applies to government action. If a private party obtains evidence, the courts will not exclude it even if the search was illegal (the defendant could always bring a civil action against the private party for trespass, etc.). As you would expect, the police can't have private citizens doing their dirty work for them; if the private party conducts an illegal search at the behest of the police, the evidence can be excluded.

Police Good Faith Exception

If the police reasonably believe that they are not acting unconstitutionally, evidence they find may still be admitted even if it is later determined that the search was unconstitutional (why discipline the police if they *reasonably* believed they were acting properly?). This usually becomes an issue where the police have a warrant that turns out to be defective for some reason. However, the police cannot rely on the "good faith exception" where:

- The affidavit in support of the warrant was so lacking in probable cause that no reasonable officer would rely on it.
- The warrant was "defective on its face"—lacks a specific address, etc.
- The officer actually lied in obtaining the warrant.

Legal Briefs

Exclusionary rule—prohibits the use of evidence obtained in violation of a defendant's rights from being used at trial to prove guilt.

Fruit of the poisonous tree—additional evidence obtained as a result of illegally obtained evidence.

Independent source—where the prosecution can prove that evidence was obtained in a way not connected to an illegal search or seizure.

Inevitable discovery—where the police would have inevitably discovered evidence without regard to any illegal search or seizure.

Impeachment exception—illegally obtained evidence can be used to impeach the defendant's testimony at trial.

Police good faith exception—if the police reasonably believe that their search or seizure was not unconstitutional (as where they have a warrant that turns out to be defective for some reason other than the police lied to obtain the warrant or it is obviously defective on its face), illegally obtained evidence might not be excluded.

Chapter 24 ——————————— ⚖

The Fourth Amendment: Arrests

"STOP RIGHT THERE! THIS IS THE POLICE! LEGS APART, HANDS BEHIND YOUR HEAD!"

An arrest? Sure, but lawyers think about this in constitutional terms as a *seizure*, which occurs anytime the police *exercise control of a person (or thing)*. The two common seizures are *arrests* and *investigatory stops*. As you know, the Fourth Amendment prohibits the government from conducting unreasonable searches and seizures, so every arrest and stop must be analyzed to see whether it was reasonable. Whether a seizure is reasonable under the Fourth Amendment depends on the scope of the seizure and the amount and strength of the evidence supporting the seizure.

Arrests

What actually constitutes an arrest is not as straightforward a question as it might seem. An arrest means the police take a person into custody for the purpose of criminal prosecution (which includes interrogation and investigation). This means either that the police applied some force to the suspect or that the suspect submitted to a police show of force. Words alone won't do it. Even if an officer thinks she's made an arrest by yelling "Stop in the name of the law!" she hasn't—there is no arrest until the officer uses or shows some physical force that causes the suspect to be under her control.

There is no specific type of force that the police must use. We're all accustomed to the image of an officer slapping cuffs on a suspect, but that is not the only way to affect an arrest. Using handcuffs may be police procedure, but any physical force that shows the suspect that she is not free to leave of her own volition would suffice (grabbing the suspect, pushing her into the back of the cruiser, blocking her from leaving a room). Again, *what the officer says or even believes* is not the issue. If the suspect is not free to leave, she *is* under arrest even if the officer never uses the word or intended to make an arrest. The test is whether under the circumstances a *reasonable person* (objective test) would feel that she was free to leave.

Presumably, Father Jack was such a reasonable person in the "Grave Doubts" episode of *The Closer* (#30). When Lieutenant Provenza's card is found in the wallet of a recently unearthed teenage gang member who was murdered fifteen years ago, Deputy Chief Brenda Johnson and crew are on the case. Their investigation eventually leads them to Father Jack, a priest who works with gang members trying to turn their lives around. Fifteen years ago, Father Jack turned in the murder weapon to the police as part of his efforts to lead gang members away from lives of crime. Yet Father Jack is none too helpful to the investigation, as he is reluctant to lose the trust of his flock. At one point, Johnson has Father Jack brought in and placed in an interview room.

When Chief Pope and a community activist confront Johnson and demand to know why she has had Father Jack arrested, Brenda says that she did *not* have Father Jack arrested. But as she rushes to speak to the Father in the interview room, she implies that he is not free to leave unless the community activist (actually the brother of the murdered gang member) tells her what he knows. Father Jack says: "You're holding me hostage?" Brenda objects to those words, but never tells Father Jack that he is free to leave.

While Deputy Chief Johnson never said the word "arrest" in connection with having the good Father brought in and might herself actually believe that she did not arrest him, it is likely that a court reviewing the circumstances would conclude that Father Jack had been arrested.

Of course, the police are not free to arrest citizens whenever they want. The police must have *probable cause* for every arrest. "Probable cause" is *information sufficient to warrant a reasonable person to believe that the suspect has committed or is committing a crime.* This is an objective test based on the circumstances of each case.

The factors that a police officer can take into account in reaching his belief that he has probable cause are varied (specific observations of the suspect, knowledge of typical criminal behavior, statements from confidential informants, etc.). There is no "magic" formula, and different judges can reach differing conclusions as to the propriety of the arrest based on similar evidence.

Although TV shows often depict the police taking suspects to the police station for questioning, the rule is that they need probable cause for an arrest to bring a person in for questioning. While the officers may try to make it seem like the suspect is going voluntarily ("Hey, it will be a lot easier if we do this downtown"), if the suspect can show that a reasonable person would have felt he had to go and could not leave once at the station, the arrest might be invalid and the interview suppressed.

Most arrests in public places are made without a warrant. The rule is that an officer may make an arrest in a public place if he has reason to believe that this person committed a felony offense (the officer need not have witnessed the felony) *or* if the person committed a misdemeanor offense in the officer's presence. It is not relevant whether the police had time to get a warrant; if either of these circumstances applies, they simply don't need any prior judicial review before making the arrest.

WHAT IS A WARRANT?

A warrant is judicial permission to do something (make an arrest, conduct a search). The idea is that it is sometimes better to have an impartial magistrate decide beforehand whether certain police activities that intrude on our personal freedoms are appropriate. To obtain an arrest warrant, the police usually present an affidavit to a judge or magistrate setting forth the facts that they believe show probable cause.

The Supreme Court has taken a different approach regarding *in-home* arrests. The rule is that in-home arrests *do* require a warrant. The reasoning is pretty straightforward; the home has traditionally been a bastion of privacy, and before the police invade it, they need to get prior approval from an impartial judge. This is supposed to protect us all from overzealous police officers. However, if the police already have probable cause to arrest someone and the suspect runs into his home, the police may enter the home and make the arrest if they do it to prevent the suspect's escape or the destruction of evidence.

What about the situation where the police have a valid arrest warrant for a suspect, but she's in the home of some third person? The police would have to get a separate search warrant for this third person's home; an arrest warrant gives the police authority to arrest the suspect only in public and in her own home, not in someone else's home.

For all the rules about arrests, the effect of an invalid arrest is actually limited. It does not prevent a later proper arrest or a subsequent conviction (although the suspect may sue the police for a violation of his constitutional rights). The only real consequence is if evidence is obtained from an illegal arrest. That evidence will be suppressed (unless the police can show "inevitable discovery" or "independent source").

SEIZED BY BULLET

Killing a fleeing suspect is perhaps the ultimate "seizure," and it also must be "reasonable." The use of deadly force is reasonable where it is necessary to prevent a *felon's* escape and the felon *threatens death or serious bodily harm* to the public. The rule is that the police cannot use deadly force against people fleeing from misdemeanors or felonies, and they can use deadly force against suspects fleeing felonies where the suspect presents a danger to the officers or the community.

Stops and Detentions

Not all seizures are arrests. The Supreme Court has recognized that in some situations the police may seize a person for a specific purpose and that the seizure may not rise to the level of an arrest. The police have the authority to *detain* a person for questioning even though they do not have probable cause to arrest the person. These are generally referred to as "investigatory stops" or "*Terry* stops" (named after the Supreme Court case that allowed them). If during the course of the stop the officer develops "probable cause," the officer can then arrest the suspect.

To make such an investigatory stop, the police must have a *reasonable suspicion* based on *articulable facts* that the person has some involvement in criminal activity. There is no specific definition of "reasonable suspicion," but it must be more than a vague or general suspicion and must be supported by some specific factors that the police can explain (as with probable cause, it need not be based on personal observations and can be based on a police broadcast, a report from an informant, etc.). On the other hand, "reasonable suspicion" is a lower standard than "probable cause" and therefore easier for the police to meet.

Speaking of lower standards, the infamous statutory rape case of Mary Kay Letourneau involved a *Terry* stop that really didn't stop anything. The relationship between Letourneau and her thirteen-year-old boyfriend, Vili Fualaau, was nearly nipped in the bud when the pair was actually caught together under suspicious circumstances in a parked car in June of 1996.

Officers on patrol came upon a car in a marina parking lot and saw Letourneau jumping into the front seat and Fualaau pretending to sleep in the backseat. The officers had a "reasonable suspicion" that some criminal activity was taking place and conducted interviews in the parking lot to determine if any "touching" had taken place. Letourneau and Fualaau convinced the officers that Fualaau was eighteen, and he denied that anything untoward had taken place. Even though they were eventually taken to the police station, Fualaau's mother told the police to release the boy to Letourneau and they drove off together (the mother later claimed that the police hadn't told her about what they thought was happening in the car).

The investigatory stop must not be longer than necessary for the officer to conduct a limited investigation based on his suspicions (the court will look at all the circumstances). If the officer reasonably believes the suspect has a weapon, he may "frisk" the suspect (conduct a limited "pat-down" of the suspect's outer clothing for signs of a weapon).

If the police have lawfully detained an automobile (for some reason court cases always use the word automobile) and have a reasonable suspicion that there may be a weapon in the automobile, they may search the areas where the weapon *could* be hidden. If they should happen to find evidence of a crime during their search for weapons (drugs, stolen goods), so be it; courts will not suppress this evidence, because the search was appropriate under the circumstances.

As for automobile stops, the rule is simple—the police have to have a reasonable, articulable suspicion that the driver has broken a traffic law, they are not allowed to stop drivers just to check licenses and registrations. However, if there is reason to believe the driver has broken a traffic law, the officer's actual motive in pulling over the car is irrelevant. These so-called "pretextual stops" are allowed even when the officer is looking for evidence of some crime other than breaking a traffic law. During a valid traffic stop, the police may lawfully order all occupants (not just the driver) out of the car (oops, automobile).

The legality of a *"Terry* stop" usually comes up during a suppression hearing where the defendant argues that the evidence found or statements given would not have come about but for an improper stop. It is then up to the police to show that they had a "reasonable, articulable" basis for making the stop.

Legal Briefs

Arrest—when the police physically take custody of a person for purposes of a criminal investigation or prosecution.

Probable cause—information sufficient to lead a reasonable person to believe that the suspect committed or is committing a crime.

Warrant—judicial permission for the police to make an arrest or conduct a search.

Terry **stop**—investigatory stop based on reasonable, articulable suspicion where the police detain but do not arrest a person.

Reasonable suspicion—more than a vague or general suspicion, but less than probable cause.

Chapter 25 ———————————— ⚖

The Fourth Amendment: Search and Seizure

In 2006, Joshua Bush carried in his head a key piece of evidence that prosecutors wanted to use to convict him of a robbery where a person was killed. The government can't force a defendant to talk about what he's thinking, so how could the prosecution possibly get at the evidence? Strangely enough, the evidence wasn't anything that Bush was *thinking*; it was a bullet actually lodged in his forehead, two inches above his eyes.

Prosecutors in Port Arthur, Texas, obtained a search warrant to extract the bullet, and Bush's lawyers fought the removal. Complicating the removal was the fact that bone had started growing around the bullet, necessitating surgery under general anesthesia. At least one hospital refused to perform the surgery, even after the warrant was issued. The case raises interesting questions about how aggressively the government can pursue evidence without violating constitutional protections against unreasonable searches and seizures.

As with arrests, searches and seizures (of things) are controlled by the Fourth Amendment so they must be *reasonable*. Unlike with arrests, though, "reasonableness" here means that the police must usually obtain a warrant before acting. That's because most arrests occur in public places, while searches and seizures generally involve an intrusion on a person's private property.

Preliminary Matters

The first thing to know about search and seizure law is that it only applies to governmental action and not the actions of private citizens. If your significant other rifles through your apartment looking for love letters to your "former" girlfriend, you have no Fourth Amendment claim against her (and you might want to change your lock). What the Fourth Amendment does cover are the police, people working for the police (informants, etc.), and public school officials.

The next important thing to know is that Fourth Amendment protections apply only to places where the person has *a reasonable expectation of privacy*. Whether a person has such an expectation will be based on factors such as ownership of the location, continuing use of the location, etc. Generally speaking, public places and things held out to the public are not going to qualify.

You might be surprised at what else courts consider to be "held out to the public," and therefore things a person has no "reasonable expectation of privacy" regarding:

- Handwriting
- The sound of a person's voice
- Telephone numbers a person dials
- Bank records

Then there's the oldest police trick in the book (at least as seen on TV)—giving the suspect a drink or cigarette and taking the cup or butt with you for the DNA evidence on it. If the suspect doesn't keep it, well by golly, he obviously didn't have a reasonable expectation of privacy in it. That's exactly what Benson and Stabler did in a *Law & Order: SVU* episode called "Pretend" (#182). Our intrepid detectives were trying to discover the real identity of a girl who had been at the center of a love triangle that resulted in one high school boy killing his best friend and romantic rival in an "extreme wrestling" match.

It turns out that the "girl," supposedly a sixteen-year-old high school student in foster care, was actually a much older woman who had conned her way into foster homes across the country. When one of her high school boyfriends paid someone to hit her with a car to keep her from testifying in court, Benson and Stabler visited her in her recovery room. After "helping" the woman by giving her a drink with a straw, Benson gives Stabler a meaningful look and walks off with the drink and straw. In the next scene they have a full dossier of the woman's life to present to Captain Cragen. Ah, the power of DNA. And the power of the police to take DNA when folks don't even know they're providing it.

Areas outside of the home and nearby structures are commonly considered to be "open fields" and are subject to police search without a warrant.

Someone growing marijuana in a field behind her house would not have Fourth Amendment protection from the police wandering by and taking notice. The police can even fly over a property and view what is in the "open fields" so long as they stay in public airspace. Courts also generally allow the police to use vision-enhancing equipment in these "fly-overs" as long as the cameras, lenses, etc., that they use are also generally available to the public (no using supersecret Department of Defense gizmos).

Standing

A key question in any search and seizure review is *who* exactly is claiming that the police made an unconstitutional search. This is known in legal terms as the question of "standing." The Supreme Court has said that a person can challenge a search only if it violates *his own* reasonable expectation of privacy. This may not sound like a big deal, but it's often a crucial question when the evidence seized was in an automobile with several passengers or a house with overnight guests, etc. Which of these people are entitled to Fourth Amendment protection?

In another *Law & Order: SVU* episode called "Guilt" (# 61), ADA Cabot argued an important standing claim in court and won, thereby securing her case against Roy Barnett, a serial pedophile.

In that show, Detectives Benson and Stabler had been unable to build a solid case against Barnett because his accuser (a young boy named Sam) tried to commit suicide after realizing that Barnett never really loved him. Fortunately, another accuser comes forward (unfortunately for the case, himself a convicted pedophile) and tells the detectives that Barnett often sent videotapes of the sexual molestations to the victims. However, the detectives can't get this crucial piece of evidence because Sam's mother refuses to let the police search her apartment. Desperate to solidify her case against Barnett, ADA Cabot later calls Benson and Stabler to Sam's apartment, implies that she has obtained a search warrant, and watches as the detectives find the tape of Sam and Barnett.

At the inevitable suppression hearing, Barnett's lawyer ably argues that the tape is the fruit of an illegal search (ADA Cabot had no warrant and no consent to search) and that the tape must be suppressed. Nevertheless, ADA Cabot is quite correct when she counters that Barnett has no standing to contest the search since he had no reasonable expectation of privacy in Sam's apartment. In fact, Cabot notes that she could illegally search any apartment in the world except Barnett's, and Barnett would have no standing to contest the search. While the judge makes clear her disdain for Cabot's actions (even promising to request that the DA's office investigate

Cabot), she also correctly rules that Barnett does not have any standing in the case and cannot challenge the admission of the tape into evidence. Of course, Cabot is reamed by her boss and suspended without pay for a month, but at least she was right about the standing issue.

Standing is usually determined on a case-by-case review of the totality of the circumstances in the case. However, there are some general rules:

- A person does have a legitimate expectation of privacy where she owns the place searched or where she is an overnight guest.
- A person does *not* have a legitimate expectation of privacy just because he owns the property seized; the location of the property at the time it was seized is the relevant question.
- Usually a person does *not* have standing to challenge a search just because he was a passenger in an automobile. If weapons and bloody clothes are found in an automobile during a search that violated *the owner's* reasonable expectation of privacy, the passenger would have no standing to challenge the evidence if it is used *against her* in a prosecution of, say, an armed assault and robbery.

Warrants

A warrant is generally required before the police may legally conduct a search or seizure. Any search or seizure undertaken without a warrant is unconstitutional *unless* it fits within one of the *exceptions to the warrant requirement*. Before we discuss those exceptions, let's look at the requirements for obtaining and executing a search warrant.

The four requirements are:

- Probable cause
- Support by oath or affirmation (testimony or affidavit from the police)
- A particular description of the place to be searched
- Must be issued by a neutral magistrate

The police must present facts to a magistrate that would allow a reasonable person to believe that the evidence sought will be found in the place or on the person to be searched. The officer applying for the warrant must provide either sworn testimony or an affidavit with these facts. It is not enough that the testimony or affidavit to conclude that there is probable cause; the magistrate must be able to make this determination independently.

The officer's testimony or affidavit may be based entirely on hearsay information (information he was told, not what the officer knows first-hand) from a victim, witness, or even a police informant. The only requirement is that the "totality of the circumstances" provides enough information to allow the magistrate to conclude that there is a reasonable probability that the evidence sought will be found in the place to be searched. This can normally be shown by statements concerning the informant's reliability and the basis for her knowledge (i.e., she was the victim; she saw the crime, etc.). Generally, the police do not have to reveal the informant's identity unless she was an eyewitness or the victim of the crime (in which case the prosecution must reveal her identity before trial).

The fact that a warrant has been issued does not automatically make a search constitutional—the defendant may challenge the validity of the warrant even after the search. A person with standing can try to show that the affidavit (or testimony) provided by the police contained a false statement, that the police intentionally or even recklessly included the false statement, and that this statement was necessary to the finding of probable cause (without it the warrant would not have been signed by the magistrate). Notice that the police must have *intentionally or recklessly* included the false statement; if the police in good faith believed the statement to be true, they have not acted intentionally or recklessly and the warrant will not be invalidated. In practice, it is very difficult for the defense to win a challenge to a warrant.

While most people are familiar with the basic idea that the police need a warrant to search a home, they may not realize that there is a *particularity* requirement for the warrant. This means that the warrant must describe with "reasonable certainty" both the place to be searched and the items to be seized.

This is commonsense stuff. If the warrant says "the apartment building," it's probably too broad; if it says "apartment 701" it's probably okay. The police must also give some specifics about *what* they are looking for. Again, common sense is the rule. If the police are after bank robbers, they might say that they believe stolen money and instruments used in the robbery (masks, guns, etc.) are in the place to be searched. The level of specificity can vary with the type of crime; a search for bank fraud might be expansively worded to include all types of records (paper, computer hard drives, photocopies, etc.), while a search for evidence of a rape would have to be more specific (perhaps certain clothes, maybe a container with a "date-rape" drug, etc.).

The final requirement is that the warrant must be issued by a "neutral" magistrate. Common sense (and the Supreme Court) says this means that the "neutral" magistrate can't be someone in the DA's office or a person who is paid for each warrant she signs.

In an episode entitled "Payback" on *Law & Order* (#313), Detectives Green and Briscoe are trying to build a case against organized crime figure Federico Righetti, who feigns insanity to escape prosecution for his crimes. Since his release from prison, Righetti has commissioned crimes (including murder) to settle old debts.

Briscoe and Green present a warrant to record Righetti's phone conversations to a sympathetic judge, Gus Stamos, who has previously dealt with Righetti. As he eats his lunch, Judge Stamos regales the detectives with a story of how he locked Righetti up years ago for contempt when Righetti showed up to his courtroom in "flip flops and a Speedo." When the detectives ask if he'll help them out, Judge Stamos says that he "doesn't like being played any more than you do by that old crook" and signs the warrant.

When it turns out that the wiretap records Righetti using code words to order a hit in a conversation with realtor Gary Stillman, Green and Briscoe arrest Stillman and charge him with the murder that occurred shortly after the phone conversation. Stillman's lawyer attacks the warrant for the wiretap, saying that since Judge Stamos had a "history of mutual animosity" with Righetti, he should not have been reviewing any warrant involving Righetti. The trial judge agrees and tosses the recorded conversation, once again leaving our intrepid ADA Jack McCoy to rebuild his case after having a key piece of evidence taken away from him (an all too frequent occurrence for McCoy).

Execution of Warrants

The police are responsible for executing search warrants. When the place to be searched is a home, the police may not have members of the media with them (remember the Robert Blake case) because the media have nothing to do with the search itself and makes the invasion of personal space unreasonable.

Even when the police have a warrant, they must "knock and announce" and be refused admittance before they can kick the door in (which is actually pretty difficult to do—they usually use a battering ram). The "knock and announce" rule applies unless the police have reason to believe that this would endanger them (armed bad guys inside) or would lead to the destruction of evidence (flushed down the toilet, for example). Recently the Supreme Court undermined the "knock and announce" requirement by ruling that evidence seized in violation of the rule does not necessarily have to be excluded.

When executing a search warrant, the police may detain persons who are at the premises in order to secure the scene, protect the officers, and allow for an orderly search. The police cannot search these persons without some probable cause to arrest them. Finally, unlike an arrest warrant, a search warrant can grow "stale" if it is not executed within a reasonable period of time.

Exceptions to the Warrant Requirement

Although the Constitution requires that all searches be reasonable, the Supreme Court has determined that this does not mean that the police must always get a warrant. There are some situations where a warrant is not required.

Search Incident to a Lawful Arrest

The police may search any person that they lawfully arrest. This means that they may search the person herself *and* the area around her where she might reach for a weapon or hide evidence (known as her "wingspan"). This search must be contemporaneous with the arrest (no going back to her apartment later and guessing where she might have been able to reach and hide the murder weapon).

When a person in an automobile is arrested, the police are allowed to search the entire interior of the car, but not the trunk (the trunk is not considered to be within any occupant's "wingspan").

Automobile Exception

If the police have probable cause to believe that an automobile has evidence or the fruits of a crime in it, they an search the automobile without a warrant. The reason for this is twofold: first, people have a lower expectation of privacy in a car than they do in their homes and, second, an automobile is mobile and it might not be there when the police return with a warrant.

The police may search the entire automobile, including the trunk and even closed containers that could physically contain the materials sought (no opening a glasses case while looking for a shotgun). The police are also allowed to tow the car to an impound lot and conduct the search there later (no contemporaneousness requirement here).

Plain View

When the police are lawfully at a location (an office, someone's home even) and they see evidence of criminal activity in "plain view," they are entitled to seize that evidence. Of course, they can't just grab a sweater they like or an ottoman that would look great back at the station house; they have to have probable cause to believe that the item is related to a criminal investigation (evidence, proceeds, etc.). If the police are executing a valid search warrant looking for stolen computers and find hand grenades on the kitchen counter, they can seize the grenades even though they were not mentioned in the warrant.

In 2006, former NBA player Lonny Baxter was arrested by uniformed Secret Service (doesn't that seem like an oxymoron—how "secret" can you be in uniform?) after shots were fired from a car about two blocks from the White House. After a witness flagged down officers and gave a description of Baxter's white SUV, the officers stopped the vehicle at a nearby intersection. They clearly had cause to stop and question Baxter, and when they did, the officers saw "spent shell casings in plain view inside the vehicle." They didn't need a warrant to search the car since the evidence was openly displayed in the car. The officers also recovered a handgun. Not unexpectedly, Baxter is no longer an NBA player.

The "plain view" exception also includes "plain smell" and "plain hear." As long as the officers are lawfully in a premises, anything they see, hear, or smell that is evidence or proceeds of a crime is subject to seizure.

Stop and Frisk Exception

When the police make a *Terry* stop (an investigative stop), they are allowed to pat down the person stopped if they reasonably believe they may find a weapon. The court will review a stop-and-frisk for reasonableness under a "totality of the circumstances" test, meaning that the court will consider all the relevant facts surrounding the officer's decision. The frisk of the detained person is essentially limited to the outer clothing unless the officer has specific information that the subject is armed (such as a tip from an informant). The officer may seize any item that she can tell just from feel is a weapon or other contraband (narcotics).

PUBLIC SCHOOLS

Public school officials do not need probable cause or a warrant to conduct a search at school. All they need is a reasonable grounds for the search. This could include things like a teacher's observation that a student has a weapon or even information from other students.

Hot Pursuit Exception

When the police are in "hot pursuit" of a fleeing felon, they may make a warrantless search and seizure. The range of the search is limited to what is necessary to prevent the felon from escaping or destroying evidence. Yes, this means the police can follow a felon inside a home, even your home, if that's what it takes to capture him.

Consent

This last exception is one that is actually fairly common, although you have to wonder about the thought process of criminals who agree to let the police search their homes, bags, and personal effects. As long as the police get voluntary and intelligent consent, they can search without a warrant.

Don't be fooled by the "intelligent" part of that rule; it does not mean that the person has to be smart or the decision a wise one, only that the person was not so mentally impaired as to be unable to make a rational decision. The police do not have to tell the person that he can refuse consent, although they are *not* allowed to tell the person that they have a warrant when in fact they do not.

The scope of the search is limited by the consent given—consent to search an apartment for a suspect would not justify opening dresser drawers. An important point is that anyone with the right to use the property (housemate, spouse, and parent) can consent to a search of the common areas (but not private areas like locked bedrooms, etc.).

In an episode called "50G Murder" on *The First 48* (#62), detectives in Dallas are investigating the robbery and murder of an elderly man in his dental clinic. A witness comes forward who says that she overheard her roommate's boyfriend and another man discussing the robbery and the shooting of the dentist. She then tells the detectives something that seems almost too good to be true—she thinks the men may have hidden the victim's wallet back in her apartment. In the next scene the detectives go to the apartment and begin searching.

With the consent to search from the witness who lives there, the detectives do not need a warrant to search the common areas. And since they are looking for a wallet, they can search pretty much anywhere that such a small item could be hidden. Eventually they notice a suspicious hole in the tile wall of the bathroom (presumably a common area). After ripping out a few more pieces of tile, the detectives find parts of the victim's wallet between the tile and the wall—just the kind of break that makes the life of a detective a whole lot easier.

Electronic Surveillance

The Supreme Court has made it clear that a search is not limited to physical inspections; any electronic surveillance by the police that intrudes on a person's reasonable expectation of privacy is a search under the Fourth Amendment and requires a warrant to be valid.

To get a warrant for electronic surveillance the police must show:

- Probable cause to believe a crime has been or will be committed
- The particular communications to be monitored
- A limited time for surveillance with an ending date
- The name(s) of the person's communications to be monitored

All electronic surveillance is governed by federal law (Title III of the Omnibus Crime Control and Safe Streets Act), and any warrant must be issued by a neutral magistrate. If the police have a valid warrant, they generally do *not* need a separate warrant to enter a premises and install the necessary equipment.

What about the average person who is recorded speaking with the subject of electronic surveillance? Have her constitutional rights been violated? The general rule is that any person using a phone assumes the risk that the person she is talking to is "unreliable" and may have given the police permission to listen to and/or record the conversation.

Shock the Conscience

Sure, "shock the conscience" would be a great name for a rock-and-roll band, but what it refers to in Fourth Amendment terms is that regardless of whether rules and tests have been met, there is a sort of catch-all rule that evidence can't be obtained by methods that make judges cringe. The police may draw blood from someone suspected of driving drunk, but they might not be able to force a suspect to undergo surgery to remove a bullet, even if the bullet is a key piece of evidence (recall Joshua Bush from the beginning of the chapter). The reasoning is that drawing blood is relatively common and low risk, while any surgery entails a more complete and dangerous invasion of a person's body (and likely involves a host of other issues, such as medical ethics).

Legal Briefs

Reasonable expectation of privacy—an analysis by the court based on factors such as ownership, use of the location, access by others; does not include things held out to the public including handwriting, sound of a person's voice, smells.

Standing—whether the search violates *this* person's reasonable expectation of privacy; determined by a review of the totality of the circumstances.

Warrant—must show probable cause, supported by oath or affirmation, with a particular place to be searched and issued by a neutral magistrate.

Exceptions to warrant requirement—circumstances where a warrant is usually not required:

Search incident of lawful arrest

Automobile exception

Plain view

Stop and frisk (*Terry* stop)

Hot pursuit

Consent

Chapter 26 ⚖️

Self-Incrimination

"I refuse to answer the question based on my Fifth Amendment rights." Admit it—you'd love a chance to say it yourself, just to show that you can't be pushed around. Of course, if you were to have any realistic chance to assert your Fifth Amendment rights, you would probably be in deep trouble. But, most people don't really understand the Fifth Amendment anyway, so who's to say that you can't use that line when you're asked why you didn't clean last night's dishes?

The Fifth Amendment

The Fifth Amendment says that "no person shall be compelled in any criminal case to be a witness against himself."

Note the reflexive voice in the wording (see, high school English class wasn't totally useless). Although it is nice to think of others, the Fifth Amendment right is *personal*; a witness can't assert the privilege because her testimony would incriminate someone else. The privilege can be asserted in *any proceeding* (criminal or civil) where the government wants to compel testimony that *could* be used against the person in a prosecution. Usually, if there is any realistic possibility that the statements could in any way be part of a chain of evidence that would incriminate the witness, the court will uphold the witness's right not to answer questions.

While the privilege can be asserted at any stage in a criminal case (interrogations, pretrial hearings, grand jury proceedings), the privilege must be asserted at the time of the questioning; there's no answering now and then later deciding to assert the privilege. Once the witness has answered, she's waived the privilege (at least as to those questions and perhaps as to the whole matter being discussed). Sitting silently won't do it—the witness has to say that she's relying on her Fifth Amendment rights (although there's no magic formula to repeat—just so long as it's understood that the witness claims the right not to answer).

Although the scope of the privilege is fairly wide ranging, only "testimonial" evidence is protected, not physical evidence. The state may compel a witness to give writing or voice exemplars or even a blood sample. The state can make a person stand in a lineup and give fingerprints. The police may need to get a warrant from a magistrate before they do any of these things, but a person usually cannot stop them by asserting her Fifth Amendment rights.

Another important point is that the privilege only applies to *compelled* testimony. The "compelled" part means that the police can't use testimony that they beat out of someone; in theory at least, this prohibition on the use of "compelled" testimony should make the police less likely to use such methods. The fact is, not only are the methods used to obtain coerced testimony frequently repulsive, but testimony given under such conditions is generally considered unreliable. People will say the darnedest things to get someone stop jolting them with electric current.

Almost any governmental or police questioning meets the standard of compulsion. Certainly being sweated in an interrogation room by team of detectives counts. But did you know that even things like filing tax returns can be considered compulsion? If you think that answering questions on your return could tend to incriminate you, you might be able to assert your Fifth Amendment right and leave them blank (but you still have to file the return). On the other hand, business papers, notes of meetings, or even diaries may be seized by the police as long as the statements in them were not coerced by the government at the time they were made.

So significant is the privilege against self-incrimination that the Supreme Court has held that the state cannot burden (or as we lawyers like to say, "chill") the exercise of the Fifth Amendment by penalizing a person who asserts it. A common way that the state *could* encumber the right is to make an issue of it at trial: "This defendant could have talked to the police during the investigation" or "He could have taken the stand here at trial and denied these charges himself, but he chose not to." The rule is that the prosecution is *not* allowed to comment in any way on the defendant's silence.

"NO ADVERSE INFERENCE" INSTRUCTION

In fact, not only is the prosecution not allowed to comment to the jury about a defendant's silence, but the defendant is commonly entitled to have the judge instruct the jury that they are to draw no adverse inference from the fact that the defendant did not testify. The idea is to remind the jury that it is the prosecution's duty to prove the elements of the charges, and that the defendant has an absolute right not to testify. Whether this instruction actually draws further attention to the fact that the "star" in the trial failed to take the stand is sometimes debated.

As important a right as the Fifth Amendment privilege is, it can be taken away by the government. Of course, it's only fair that the government give something in exchange. What the government gives in exchange is *immunity from prosecution*. Remember, the privilege applies only where there is a possibility of incrimination based on the witnesses' statements. Take away that possibility and you take away the rationale for the privilege. For the same reason, the privilege does not apply where the statute of limitations for the crime has elapsed.

IMMUNITY

There are two types of immunity the government (prosecutor) can give a witness: (1) use immunity—which means that the state can't use the testimony against the witness in any prosecution; and (2) transactional immunity—which means the witness can't be prosecuted for any actions mentioned in the testimony. Transactional immunity is broader, but the government generally only has to offer use immunity to compel testimony from a witness.

Confessions

On September 7, 1988, Marty Tankleff, then seventeen years old, woke up in his suburban Long Island home ready for the first day of his senior year in high school. He went downstairs and discovered his father, Seymour Tankleff, lying on the floor, battered and bloody. Marty then found his mother, Arlene Tankleff, dead on her bedroom floor. Marty called 911. An ambulance rushed Seymour to the hospital.

The lead detective on the case, James McCready, was immediately bothered by Marty's affect when the police first talked to him. According to McCready, Marty was calm and composed, not grieving as one might expect of a teenager whose parents had just been brutally attacked. Marty said that his father's business partner, Jerry Steurman, who had been at a poker game at the Tankleffs' the night before and who owed Seymour a lot of money, could have been involved. Marty agreed to go to the police station and speak further with the detectives.

For hours Marty sat in a small windowless room without a lawyer and talked with the police. McCready and his partner repeatedly told Marty that they knew he did it and that things would be okay if he just told them that he killed his mother and sent his father to the hospital. Marty did not admit to the attacks. Then McCready left the room and when he returned, he told Marty that Seymour had been injected with adrenaline and had come out of his coma. Seymour, Detective McCready said, had told investigators that Marty had committed the crime. In fact, McCready was lying; he had not even spoken to Seymour.

Later, Marty, who says that his father never lied to him, admitted that his father's "statement" made him begin to doubt his own memory. He thought that maybe he had actually attacked his parents and then blacked out. Marty says that he was scared, disoriented, and confused, and that he finally told the police what they wanted to hear—he had attacked his parents. McCready prepared a written statement in which Marty admitted to the crime, although Marty never signed it.

Marty almost immediately recanted, but he was arrested and eventually charged with two murders (Seymour later died from his injuries). Although there was little physical evidence, Marty's confession was used against him and he was convicted. Years later, of his confession Marty said: "It's like having an eighteen-wheeler driving on your chest and you believe that the only way to get that weight off your chest is to tell the police whatever they want to hear." Even admit to brutal murders he now says he didn't commit.

Marty Tankleff's story was featured on the CBS show *48 Hours: Mystery* ("Prime Suspect," April 2004). His story was also "ripped from the headlines" in a *Law & Order: Criminal Intent* episode called "The Good" (#111), in which a character named Kevin Colmar is tricked into confessing to murdering his parents in their suburban home (although he claims not to remember the crime).

TRUE OR FALSE QUESTION

If Marty Tankleff did make a "false confession," he wouldn't be the first person to do so. Although it doesn't fit with our understanding of human behavior, there have been plenty of false confessions in the history of American criminal justice. More than *200 people* confessed to kidnapping the Lindbergh baby. The Central Park jogger rape case was reopened years after five young men were convicted based on their videotaped confessions. More recently, John Mark Karr appeared to confess to one of the most notorious unsolved crimes of all time, the brutal murder of six-year-old JonBenet Ramsey.

Some false confessions are voluntary and seem to stem from a desire to find a way into the public eye or appear more "powerful" than the person really is. Some false confessions are the result of wanting to take the fall for a loved one or a comrade in crime. Others have the earmarks of overzealous police interrogation techniques.

One case that is markedly similar to the Tankleff case involved eighteen-year-old Peter Reilly, who found his dead mother in the apartment they shared. He denied any involvement at first, but after the police pressed him for eight more hours and said that he had failed an "infallible" lie detector test, Reilly signed a complete confession admitting to the crime. He was convicted of manslaughter although there was little or no physical evidence linking him to the crime. Three years later his conviction was overturned based on new evidence and the judge's finding that that Reilly's confession had been coerced.

The admissibility at trial of a confession (or other incriminating statements by the defendant) involves analysis under the *Fourteenth Amendment*, which protects against involuntary confessions, the *Sixth Amendment*, which gives defendants rights regarding the assistance of counsel, and the *Fifth Amendment*, which gives defendants rights against testimonial self-incrimination. As you can tell from all the "amendments" being thrown around here, criminal law takes this confession business seriously.

The Fourteenth Amendment

The first step in looking at a confession is to see if it was made *voluntarily*. The confession must have been a "free choice" by the defendant. Whether the defendant spoke voluntarily is assessed on a *subjective* basis considering all the circumstances surrounding the giving of the confession. Courts look at a variety of factors concerning *this particular defendant* including her age, level of education, experiences with the criminal justice system, etc. Courts also look at the means used in the interrogation (length of interviews, number of interviews, physical conditions of interview room) as well as the means used by the interrogators (promises, lies, etc.).

LET'S GO TO THE VIDEOTAPE . . .

. . . Or not. Since most states ask the court to weigh a variety of factors (age, education, experience with the law, length of interview, etc.) in deciding whether a confession was made voluntarily, it would seem to make sense to have the police videotape the interrogations whenever practicable (excluding times, for example, when an interrogation takes place at the scene, etc.). However, only a few states require videotaping. That number may increase, although some law enforcement agencies are opposed to the idea for a number of reasons (cost, practicality).

As Marty Tankleff discovered, deception by the police does not render a confession inadmissible. When McCready left the room and pretended he had spoken with Marty's gravely injured father, he was doing nothing more than trying to trick Marty into believing that he, Marty, had been identified by a witness. In that situation, it is difficult to conceive of a more powerfully persuasive lie than the one McCready concocted; nevertheless, courts will generally not find that a confession given in these circumstances was involuntary. Although Marty was only seventeen at the time of the murders, confessions made by a minor (even someone younger than Marty) are not automatically considered involuntary.

It is important to remember that even if a court rules that a confession was made voluntarily and is therefore admissible, the issue is not completely dead. Marty was entitled at trial to present evidence and testimony about the circumstances surrounding the confession and argue that it should not be given any credence. Apparently, in his case the jury decided that his confession was worth believing.

Sixth Amendment Right to Counsel

Even if a confession is made voluntarily, it will not be admissible at trial if the statement was taken in violation of a defendant's Sixth Amendment right. The Sixth Amendment says that in criminal prosecutions, the defendant has a right to counsel. The idea is that a person should not have to navigate the dangerous shoals of the criminal justice system without a guide. The key to understanding this right is to focus on when it becomes available to the defendant.

This right to counsel applies only at the outset of "adversary judicial proceedings," i.e., after an indictment in most cases. After an indictment, the police can only question a defendant in the presence of his counsel (unless the defendant has made a voluntary and knowing waiver of his right to counsel). If the police violate this rule, the confession will not be admissible. Remember, though, a defendant has no Sixth Amendment right to counsel prior to an indictment, even if he is being questioned by the police after having been arrested (although he may have a *Fifth Amendment* right to counsel during a custodial interrogation).

Unless a defendant already has a lawyer, she must request one (no magic words need to be said as long as he makes it known to the police that he would like counsel). The right is "offense specific," meaning that the defendant must request a lawyer each time he is charged with a crime. As a result, if a defendant requests a lawyer for one offense for which he has been indicted (say kidnapping), he may not be questioned about that offense without his lawyer but may be questioned about separate crimes (perhaps a series of bank robberies) for which he has not been charged or for which he has not requested counsel.

Fifth Amendment Right to Counsel

The basic premise of the famous *Miranda* warnings (from the Supreme Court case of the same name) is that a custodial police interrogation is inherently coercive. Just the fact that the government (in the form of the police) has seized a person and is asking questions puts real pressure on the person. In an effort to level the playing field, the Supreme Court has said that prior to any custodial interrogation, the police must inform the person of her rights, warn her about what may happen if she waives those rights, and obtain a waiver of those rights before getting a confession. If the police fail to be properly informative to their suspect, any confession will be excluded from the prosecution's case at trial.

MIRANDA RIGHTS

The actual words of the famous *Miranda* warning ("You have the right to remain silent; anything you do say can be used against you; you have the right to an attorney; if you cannot afford one, one will be provided for you.") are not anywhere in the Constitution, nor are these words required by the Constitution. Nevertheless, most police departments use something exactly like what you hear on TV.

Since *Miranda* only applies to custodial interrogations, an important question is, when is a person in custody? The basic answer is when he is not free to leave. This could mean what is called a "formal arrest" (you know, officers in tuxedos, a gracious request to be seated at an interview table covered with fine white linen). Or it could mean some intrusive level of restraint on a person's liberty to move (so even where the police don't call it an "arrest" but they restrain a person's movement, *Miranda* would apply).

The basic test a court will use in deciding whether a person was in custody (and *Miranda* applies) is whether under the circumstances a *reasonable person* would feel that he was not free to leave the situation. This usually would not include something like a routine traffic stop, where a reasonable person would recognize the limited duration of the restrictions on his liberty. This is an objective test and requires a close look at the details of the interrogation (where it took place, when, how many officers, public area or home, etc.).

THE FRIENDLY CELLMATE

Miranda applies only to interrogations where the person would be intimidated or coerced by the fact that the police are questioning her. It makes sense that if the person is not aware that questions are being asked by the police, *Miranda* does not apply. That's why *Miranda* warnings don't have to be given by a cellmate working for the police who questions a defendant.

Miranda applies only to custodial *interrogation*. If the police approach a person who spontaneously bursts out with "I don't know why I did it!"—no interrogation has taken place and the statement can be used at trial, even though the person was not given his *Miranda* warnings before making the statement. However, after arresting this knucklehead, the police would have to "Mirandize" him before asking any follow-up questions.

The Supreme Court knows that police officers can be tricky sometimes, so it has said that "interrogation" is not limited to direct questioning, but can cover any type of behavior likely to bring an incriminating response from a suspect. This could include things like arresting officers having a conversation between themselves where they speak in a way specifically designed to draw out a response from the suspect. However, *Miranda* does not apply to routine booking questions (name, address, etc.).

A suspect may terminate police questioning by either telling the police that he wishes to remain silent *or* by requesting counsel. The analysis of any further questioning differs depending on which Fifth Amendment right he invokes.

Where the suspect invokes his *right to remain silent*, the police must stop questioning him. Period. However, the police may later (hours later) come back, reread him his *Miranda* warnings, and try to question him about a *different crime.*

If the suspect invokes his right to counsel (universally referred to on shows from *Law & Order* to *CSI: NY* as "lawyering up"), the police must stop questioning until the suspect has had a chance to confer with counsel (who will inevitably warn him not to speak to the police). The police may not even question the suspect about an unrelated crime as they can where the suspect has merely invoked his right to silence.

A request to talk to a lawyer has to be unambiguous and clear enough that a reasonable police officer would understand the words used to be a request for counsel. The old "maybe I should talk to a lawyer first" probably doesn't cut it.

CONSEQUENCES

The consequence for either failing to give a defendant her *Miranda* warnings or for violating the exercise of those rights is simple—the confession is suppressed. And not just in *Law & Order* episodes. Consider the infamous 2006 case of John Evander Couey, arrested for kidnapping, assaulting, and murdering nine-year-old Jessica Lunsford in Florida (this was the case where Couey, who lived in a mobile home near where Jessica lived, buried her alive in the yard after assaulting her). Couey's taped confession was thrown out by the trial judge because the police ignored Couey's request to speak to an attorney during the interrogation. The judge called this "a material and a profound violation of one of the most bedrock principles of criminal law."

Of course, a defendant can waive his *Miranda* rights and speak to the police without his lawyer. It is up to the government, though, to show the trial court that the waiver was "knowing and intelligent." This simply requires that the defendant heard the rights in language he could understand (even if a translator is required). The police are not under any obligation to explain in detail what the rights mean or how the criminal justice system works.

The court will look at all the circumstances surrounding the confession, including the defendant's age, level of education, physical condition, etc., in determining whether the waiver was knowing and intelligent. Generally, as long as the police can show that the warnings were given, they don't have much difficulty meeting the test (although waiving your rights and making incriminating statements or a confession doesn't seem very intelligent).

The waiver does not have to be in written form, although a waiver signed by the defendant is persuasive. If the defendant makes a confession even though his lawyer is present, a court would be hard pressed to find that the confession was made in violation of *Miranda*. In the absence of a signed piece of paper, a court might even infer a knowing and intelligent waiver where the police can show that they gave the *Miranda* warnings and the defendant spoke anyway; it all depends on the circumstances of the particular case.

HANDCUFFING THE POLICE?

The famous *Miranda* decision has been heavily criticized since it came out of the Supreme Court. An early and frequent criticism was that it would "handcuff" the police, since any right-thinking person would obviously shut up and immediately ask for a lawyer, thereby robbing the police (no pun intended) of a valuable crime-solving technique. However, as almost any police officer can tell you, suspects frequently waive their rights. This just goes to show that it is difficult to predict human behavior, and also that you don't have to be that bright to be a criminal.

Legal Briefs

No adverse inference—the jury is not allowed to draw an adverse inference against the defendant if she does not testify.

Use immunity—given to a witness so that the state cannot use the witness's statements against him in a prosecution.

Transactional immunity—given to a witness so that the state cannot prosecute the witness regarding the subject ("transaction") covered by the testimony.

Confessions—must be voluntary (Fourteenth Amendment); the defendant must be given access to counsel if made after the outset of "adversary judicial proceedings" (Sixth Amendment); defendant must be given *Miranda* warnings (Fifth Amendment) if questioning is "custodial."

Chapter 27 ⚖

Pretrial Proceedings

An awful lot happens between an arrest and a trial (if there is one). The exact form of these "pretrial proceedings" varies from state to state, although all states must follow certain constitutionally mandated measures. There will be several hearings for a variety of purposes, such as reviewing probable cause and setting bail (if appropriate). Some of these hearings may be combined, depending on the timeline of the case itself and the particular practices of each state.

Preliminary Hearing

This is sometimes referred to as a "*Gerstein* hearing," after a Supreme Court case that established the outlines of this procedure. The basic reason for this hearing is for judicial review of the probable cause that was the basis for the arrest and detention. Where the defendant is released following her arrest, no *Gerstein* hearing is required because there is no longer any detention (although the defendant will be given a date to return to court for trial, if any).

In many cases there has already been a review of the probable cause basis for arresting the defendant, in which case there is no need to hold a *Gerstein* hearing. For example, if the police obtained an arrest warrant for the defendant, a magistrate has *already* found probable cause to arrest and detain the defendant. Likewise, a grand jury indictment prior to the arrest establishes the probable cause for the arrest, and no *Gerstein* hearing is held.

In any case, where there is no arrest warrant and no indictment, the defendant has a Fourth Amendment right to a hearing to determine if there is probable cause to detain her. When required, a *Gerstein* hearing generally must be held within forty-eight hours of the arrest. The hearing itself is straightforward and usually fairly simple. It is a *nonadversarial* hearing, which means that the defendant has no right to cross-examine the witnesses. The prosecutor essentially lays out the facts the police relied upon in making the arrest. The prosecutor usually tries to present the minimum amount of evidence and testimony to accomplish this (why let the defendant hear the whole case in advance?). The prosecutor may even rely on hearsay evidence that might not be admissible at trial.

Initial Appearance

This is what you see in all those *Law & Order* episodes where the cranky judge presides over what looks for all intents and purposes like a cattle-call (this comes in the second half of the show, after the dastardly deed, the wisecrack by Briscoe or his successors, and the investigation). Even if there is no need for a *Gerstein* hearing (there was an arrest warrant or indictment), the defendant must be presented to a judge within seventy-two hours of the arrest. The defendant will stand in front of the judge, who will take care of some housekeeping matters (informing the defendent of her rights, making sure she has a lawyer, etc.). This hearing is often combined with a bail hearing, as where the *Law & Order* judge inquires as to the state's position on bail by saying something like "Miss Carmichael, the people on bail?"

Bindover Hearing

A bindover hearing reviews the prosecutor's decision to charge the defendant. Unlike a *Gerstein* hearing, this is an adversarial hearing; the defendant is entitled to counsel and may cross-examine prosecution witnesses and present her own witnesses and evidence. The burden is on the prosecution to prove that there is some evidence of each element of the crime charged. The defendant may waive this hearing and it is not required when the defendant has already been indicted.

Bail

The Eighth Amendment and some state constitutions say that "excessive bail shall not be required." It is very important to keep in mind that the purpose of bail is to assure that the defendant will appear at trial (and all pretrial proceedings). Obviously every defendant is "presumed innocent" (hey, that would be a great title for a book, and a movie starring Harrison Ford), and bail is meant to insure that defendants are not punished before conviction. Bail should be set no higher than is necessary to convince the defendant to come back for the trial. In most states, if the defendant thinks that bail is excessive, he can immediately appeal the judge's decision.

In thinking about bail, remember that the odiousness of the crime should not be a factor. An accused child molester who does not appear to be a flight risk may properly receive a lower bail than a petty thief with a history of failing to appear for trials. However, sometimes the nature of the crime and the potential punishment may be a major factor in a bail decision. For example, if a defendant is "facing the needle," as they say on TV shows, it is not all that likely that he would return for trial no matter how high the bail. In that case, the defendant may be *held without bail*.

Some states, and the federal government, have passed "preventive detention" statutes that allow courts to deny bail to defendants who are seen as dangerous to society. Usually these statutes also require an expedited trial date for anyone held in preventive detention.

The usual system for pretrial bail is based on dollars and cents. The idea is that the possibility of a big financial hit to the defendant (or her family and friends) will convince her to come back to face the music. If the defendant does not have the money, she can turn to a bail bondsman who will post the money for a fee (perhaps 10 percent of the total). This system obviously favors those with assets and has been frequently criticized as unfair. Recently, more courts have been using other bail options such as property bonds (putting a house up instead of cash) and even things like releasing the defendant directly into another's custody or some form of house arrest.

Indictment and Information

Many states and the federal government require indictments for all felony cases. An indictment is an accusation written by the prosecutor that charges a person with a crime. The indictment is submitted to a grand jury (called a "charging grand jury"), which reviews any evidence presented by the prosecutor and decides if there is probable cause to believe that the person charged has committed the crime. If the grand jury supports the indictment, they will mark it as a "true bill"; if not, they will mark it "no true bill," and the person will not be charged.

Some states do not use grand juries, instead relying on the prosecutor to file a written accusation of the crime called an "information." An information can also be used in "grand jury" states where the defendant waives his right to an indictment. In most states, an information is used to charge misdemeanors. The information must be specific enough that the defendant knows what the charge against him is. Typically the prosecutor will parrot the wording of the statute she believes the defendant violated. Some states may also require basic information such as dates, times, locations, etc.

Grand Juries

Grand juries are interesting because they operate very differently from the open, adversarial mechanisms of most of our criminal law system. Their original purpose was to be a buffer between the king and the people. Now they are often considered a prosecutor's best friend.

Grand jury proceedings are *secret*, even from the defendant. Although the members of the grand jury are in charge of deciding a matter of grave importance to the defendant, in most states the defendant has no right to know that the grand jury is considering charges and she has *no right to appear*. Generally speaking, grand jury proceedings are also kept secret from the public.

The prosecutor has wide latitude in deciding what evidence to show the grand jury members before asking them to vote on the indictment. The prosecutor has largely unrestricted power to subpoena witnesses to testify. She can decide to grant witnesses immunity and compel their testimony. In most states, a witness is not allowed to have a lawyer present during testimony, and there is no judge in the grand jury room. The prosecutor can use hearsay evidence and even evidence obtained illegally (say a weapon recovered in an illegal search that will be inadmissible at trial).

Whether the prosecutor shows conflicting evidence to the grand jury is up to her good judgment (although she may have to if required by the constitution or a state statute). Finally, a grand jury vote need not be unanimous. If there are, say, 23 grand jurors, a simple majority of 12 could return a true bill (which might tell the prosecutor something about the strength of her evidence).

In theory, grand jurors are independent and are allowed to ask questions of witnesses or even call witnesses that they wish to question. In practice they usually only hear from witnesses the prosecution presents and listen only to the prosecution's questioning of the witnesses. There's a saying that a prosecutor could indict "a ham sandwich," which, while perhaps exaggerating things, underlines the point that a grand jury indictment is well short of a conviction.

The grand jurors are selected from the same pool as are trial jurors ("petit jurors"). They often sit for a month at a time and hear whatever cases the prosecution brings to them during that time. On rare occasions grand juries are impaneled for a long-term investigation (think organized crime or political corruption cases) and may sit for anywhere from six months to years.

Prosecution's Obligation to Disclose

While the grand jury process is clearly tilted in favor of the prosecution, there are certain pretrial matters that cut in favor of the accused. One of these is the obligation of the prosecution to disclose evidence favorable to the defense.

Although our system is an adversarial one where we rely on conflict to produce the basis for the decisions of fact, we don't allow unfair fighting, especially by the prosecution. The Due Process Clause requires that the government disclose to the defense any exculpatory evidence. This is known as the "*Brady* rule," after the Supreme Court case of that name.

The definition of "exculpatory evidence" is quite broad; courts consider pretty much anything that could undermine the prosecution's case as exculpatory. Things like deals the prosecution makes with witnesses must be disclosed (as they could show bias by the witness in exchange for a good deal). Even something like the identity of a "confidential" informant may have to be disclosed if the identity could be helpful to the defense.

Where evidence favorable to the defense has *not* been turned over prior to trial, the defendant can appeal a conviction on the basis that the evidence would "undermine confidence" in the verdict; she does not have to show that she would have been acquitted. The defendant does not have to have specifically requested the evidence since the burden is on the prosecutor to disclose. And the prosecutor cannot remain willfully ignorant in order to evade her responsibility to disclose exculpatory evidence; she has a *duty to find* exculpatory evidence in the possession of the police and other governmental agents.

In some cases the defendant may have to disclose information to the prosecution. For example, some states require notice if the defendant intends to rely on an alibi defense (thereby giving the prosecution time to investigate the alibi evidence). Some states even require each side to show their evidence to the other side before trial. This is known as "reciprocal discovery" and is designed to prevent unfair surprises for either side at trial.

Legal Briefs

Preliminary hearing—*Gerstein* hearing; judicial review of probable cause for arrest and detention.

Bail—financial security given by the defendant to insure that she returns to court; not meant to punish defendants accused of heinous or violent crimes.

Indictment—a "true bill" returned by a grand jury finding probable cause that the defendant committed a felony.

Grand jury—group of jurors that hears evidence from prosecutor and votes on indictments.

Information—written accusation filed by prosecutor in place of indictment; usually for misdemeanors and in some states felonies.

***Brady* rule**—requires the prosecution to turn over to the defense any exculpatory information.

Chapter 28 ⚖

Trial

On the night of a big high school football game in a small Texas town, a man kidnaps three high school girls and imprisons them in a small, unfurnished, and windowless basement. The girls, all friends and teammates on their varsity soccer team, are understandably traumatized and frightened. Their kidnapper gives them no food or water. He tells them only one thing—two of them will come out alive after they kill the third. At first the girls are utterly disgusted at the very idea, but as several days pass in the cold with no sustenance of any kind, two of the girls agree to kill the third girl, who is sick and barely conscious.

They yell to their kidnapper that they have made their decision, and he simply tosses two hammers into the room. Realizing that he means for *them* to kill their friend, the girls are stunned. Suddenly the sick girl rises up, grabs a hammer, and slays one of the two girls who were planning to kill her.

The kidnapper keeps his word and releases the two surviving girls on their sixth day of captivity. They are scarred for life, but they give the police and FBI enough information to capture the kidnapper inside the basement. He admits to everything on the scene and says he did it to get back at the parents of the girls, whom he has known since high school and whom he says had treated him badly.

Everyone can probably agree that this is one sick bastard. But, as we all know, even this fictional character from the 2006 episode of *Criminal Minds* called "North Mammon" deserves a fair trial. That is as American as high school football in Texas.

A Fair Trial

A defendant has a right to a fair and impartial trial. This is not to be mistaken for the right to a *perfect* trial; trials are human endeavors and mistakes are inevitably going to happen. The key is to have an impartial judge to evaluate and correct if possible any errors at trial and an impartial jury to weigh the evidence.

Obviously the judge cannot have any personal bias that would skew her rulings for either the defense or the prosecution. In some states there are procedures for either side to challenge a judge assigned to a case on grounds of some type of personal bias. Judges may also recuse themselves from cases where they have some connection that might make it appear that they are biased toward one side or the other.

The defendant also has a right to a jury that is free from unfair pressures or influences. Typical issues that might come up are that a juror has some connection with law enforcement or some personal connection with a prosecution witness. Unfair pressures or influences might also include having television cameras in the courtroom. Either the defense or prosecution (or both) might argue that televising the trial will make it difficult for the jurors to reach a fair and impartial verdict (they might be swayed by how they think the public will react to their decision, etc.).

The usual rule is that a court may allow trial proceedings to be televised as long as the televising does not interfere with the jury's ability and willingness to consider fairly all the evidence.

Where there has been a great deal of pretrial publicity that has potentially prejudiced all the potential jurors in an area, the defendant may even ask to have the trial moved to a different and presumably less hostile area (known in legal circles as a "change of venue"). If the defendant requests a change of locale, he will have to show that the pretrial publicity has affected the potential jurors' ability to fairly weight the evidence (as where a taped interview of the defendant confessing has been aired on local television).

CHANGE OF VENUE

Excessive pretrial publicity that might prejudice potential jurors against the defendant may lead the judge to order that the trial be held in a different part of the state, where the case has presumably attracted less attention. In today's Internet and Court TV world, that is probably becoming an increasingly common problem without a very good solution; it seems that everyone with a computer or TV could be exposed to the details of just about any notorious case.

The Jury

The primary reasons for jury trials are that they allow the public to participate in the criminal process and serve as a buffer against unfair prosecutions by the state. A defendant has a right to a jury trial in all cases where the *possible* penalty is more than six months in prison. However, the jury right does not apply where the defendant faces multiple misdemeanors (each with a possible sentence of less than six months), and he could be given a combined sentence of more than six months.

Surprisingly, there are not always twelve jurors in a criminal trial. In federal court there generally must be twelve jurors, but there is no requirement that a state jury have twelve members. The Supreme Court has said that a state jury of as few as *six* members is acceptable.

Also, unlike what you are accustomed to seeing on TV and reading in the news, a jury's verdict does *not* always have to be unanimous. States are allowed to use nonunanimous verdicts (11-1, 10-2, even 9-3, but probably not 8-4) if they desire, although the Supreme Court has said that a six-person jury must return a unanimous verdict. Critics of the nonunanimous verdicts argue that dissenting votes represent reasonable doubt and, for example, a 10-2 vote to convict violates the requirement that the prosecution prove all elements of the crime beyond a reasonable doubt. Nevertheless, nonunanimous verdicts are constitutional.

We all learned that a defendant is entitled to a "jury of his peers," which the Supreme Court has said means a jury selected from a representative "cross-section" of the defendant's community. A defendant may claim a violation of this right if a particular group is excluded from the *venire* (the larger collection of jurors from which the jury is selected). As to the jury itself, the defendant is *not* entitled to have proportional representation of all groups.

Selecting a Jury

Methods for selecting a jury vary widely from state to state based on local practice and tradition.

A common method for drafting jurors is to draw them at random from a public list such as voting rolls. While it used to be widespread practice to exclude some people based on the pressing nature of their job (teachers, doctors, firefighters, at-home parents), their connection to law enforcement (police personnel, judges), or for their well-known inability to speak the truth (politicians), most of these "exemptions" have been eliminated.

The clerk of the court (or some other court official) then sends a large group of jurors (called the venire, or jury pool) to the courtroom. The prosecution and the defense are then allowed to question the jurors to see if they can be fair and impartial in this particular case. This process is usually called *voir dire,* which is French for "wild guess"—actually it means "to speak the truth." In some states the judge will conduct all the questioning.

The lawyers (or judge) will ask questions designed to bring out a prospective juror's bias about anything relevant to the case (feelings about violence, drug use, law enforcement, race of the defendant or witnesses, having been a victim of a similar crime, etc.). If it becomes clear that a prospective juror is unfit to serve (cannot understand English well enough, has been drinking, has personal knowledge of the case or anyone involved), the juror will be excused *for cause* on a request by either side. These "strikes for cause" are usually unlimited.

During *voir dire,* the lawyers commonly are allowed a certain number of "peremptory strikes" (between 10 and 20 is common). Peremptory strikes allow the lawyers to strike (remove) a juror for any reason, whether rational *or* irrational. This allows the lawyers to remove potential jurors who "look at them funny" or seem "disinterested," or, worse yet, "hostile." Peremptory strikes can also be exercised to remove those jurors who don't fit the lawyer's notion of the type of juror she wants on the case (in a complex trial, a lawyer might strike jurors with little formal education; a defense lawyer might want writers and artists if she plans to present an especially creative case, etc.).

If it is a sensationalized case or involves a very serious potential penalty (like the death penalty) or both, jury selection can be a lengthy process. When Aaron McKinney was charged with the brutal 1998 murder of Matthew Shepard and faced the death penalty, the court estimated that jury selection would take up to *two weeks.* That's a lot of careful questioning by the lawyers and painstaking analysis of juror responses.

Since *voir dire* is the first time the lawyers see the jurors, it is also their first opportunity to lay the foundation of their cases. Normally a judge won't allow a lot of argument to the jurors, but lawyers can generally get across the essence of their case with questions ostensibly designed to probe the jurors' feelings about elements of the trial.

For example, in the Matthew Shepard case, prosecutors contended that McKinney and his friend Russell Henderson met Shepard at a bar, pretended to be gay, and lured Shepard to McKinney's truck, where Shepard was beaten, robbed, and subsequently tied to a fence and left to die in the Wyoming cold. The case caused national outrage about crimes against homosexuals, and the issue of "gay bashing" was all over the news for months before the trial.

During jury selection the prosecutor did not even mention Shepard's sexual orientation or anything else that would indicate that this was a "hate crime" (perhaps because the prosecution did not want to give any credence to an anticipated defense that McKinney killed Shepard in a "gay panic" after Shepard made a pass at him). And McKinney's defense lawyer took an even more surprising tack during jury selection. He told potential jurors that McKinney was responsible for Shepard's death, but told them that to understand McKinney's actions they would have to understand his abuse of drugs and alcohol and his mental health problems. Remember, this is all before the trial actually started.

THE RIGHT MAN/WOMAN FOR THE JOB

There are as many theories of what type of jurors are best for what type of cases as there are lawyers trying cases. Some general rules sound like they are based on "armchair" psychology, others are often not much more than thinly veiled prejudices (women will vote with their emotions, white men tend to be conservative, etc.). Not many (if any) of these "theories" stand up to scrutiny.

Race/Gender Issues

Lawyers are not free to use peremptory challenges to exclude jurors because of their race or gender. The Equal Protection Clause forbids it. The question, of course, is how to prove that, say, a prosecutor was basing a strike on race or gender when the strikes can be used for pretty much any other reason at all. After all, couldn't the prosecutor just make up some other rational or even irrational reason for using a peremptory strike?

He could. However, there is a procedure in place for the defense to challenge a strike they believe was made because of race or gender. It is called a *Batson* challenge, from the Supreme Court case that established it. There are three steps to the process:

- the defense must show facts that raise an inference that a juror was excluded based on race or gender (perhaps a statistical analysis of the race/gender of jurors excluded)
- if the court decided that an inference has been raised, the prosecution must present a race/gender-neutral basis for the exclusion (doesn't have to be rational, just believable)

- the court then decides whether to accept the prosecution's explanation.

Keep in mind that it is also illegal for the *defense* to exclude a juror based on race or gender. If the prosecution believes this has happened, they make a *reverse Batson* challenge and follow the same procedure outlined above.

Death Penalty

Courts cannot exclude jurors simply because they are opposed to the death penalty. The real question is whether this opposition would prevent the juror from performing her duties to follow the instructions from the judge and carry out her oath as a juror. A juror who says that she will absolutely not return a verdict that results in a death penalty may properly be excluded (here, the juror has affirmatively indicated that she will not follow the judge's instructions).

What about a juror who says that she will *automatically* give the death penalty upon a guilty verdict? The same reasoning applies—she will be excluded because she has said that she will not be able to follow the judge's instructions to consider mitigating factors, etc.

Waiving a Jury Trial

A jury trial is a right not an obligation. A defendant may waive his right to a jury trial as long as he does it intelligently. Typically there would a hearing where the judge would explain the consequences of waiving the right to a jury trial. In cases where the defendant might look like a scumbag but have a technical or purely legal defense, he might well want to have a judge deciding the facts instead of an impressionable panel of his peers that might convict just because they don't like him.

Inconsistent Verdicts

Often a jury will be asked to bring back not one but several verdicts against a single defendant (as in one, not unmarried). What if the verdicts don't make sense when considered together—say, where a defendant is convicted of one felony but acquitted of a related and seemingly logically connected second felony?

As you undoubtedly know, things do not have to make sense to be legal. The usual reasoning is that since no one knows how the jurors arrived at either verdict, it is not possible to determine on which verdict they erred, so no inquiry is made and the verdicts stand as delivered.

Legal Briefs

Right to jury trial—where the possible penalty is more than six months in prison; not an obligation, and the defendant may waive a jury trial (as long as the waiver is intelligent).

Unanimity—not required in all cases (10-2 verdicts are allowed); required with six-person juries.

Voir dire—"to speak the truth"; process where judge or the lawyers question prospective jurors.

Strike for cause—where a prospective juror is disqualified from serving on the jury because of a specific reason (knowledge of case or witnesses, inability to follow instructions, etc.).

Peremptory strike—allows the lawyers to remove a prospective juror from the pool for almost any reason at all; improper to base strike on race, gender.

Batson **challenge**—where one side challenges the peremptory strike of the other side as being based on an improper reason (race or gender).

Inconsistent verdicts—multiple verdicts in a single case do not have to be logically consistent.

Chapter 29

⚖

Right to Counsel

A defendant has the right to counsel under the Fifth and Sixth Amendments. The Fifth Amendment right applies to custodial interrogations. The Sixth Amendment right applies at all *critical stages* of a prosecution after formal charges have been filed (from a defendant's point of view, are there any *non*-critical stages of a prosecution?). Basically this means that once charges have been filed, a defendant has the right to counsel at line-ups, interrogations, psychiatric evaluations, arraignments, and pretrial hearings. Also, where there is a conviction, the defendant is constitutionally entitled to counsel at sentencing hearings and at his first appeal (after that, it's up to the state to decide if he is entitled to counsel for subsequent appeals).

Not every defendant has the financial resources of OJ Simpson or Martha Stewart, so in many states the court is allowed to provide other assistance to a defendant in addition to a lawyer. Depending on the nature of the charge and the prosecution's evidence, the court might pay for a defense investigator, medical expert, etc. Typically, of course, the defendant would have to show that she lacks the financial means to pay for these services herself.

Waiver of Right to Counsel

It's one thing to represent yourself to fight a speeding ticket; it's another thing altogether to go it alone with a more serious charge. But it is your right—even if you may not be in your right mind.

In his 1999 trial, the so-called "Unabomber," Theodore Kaczynski, asked to represent himself on the afternoon before his trial was set to begin.

Authorities believed Kaczynski was responsible for sixteen mail and package bombs that killed three people and injured 23 others between 1978 and 1995. Actually, the pretrial proceedings had been going on for months, but Kaczynski made his request at the last minute because of an ongoing tactical dispute with his attorneys. Kaczynski was concerned that his lawyers planned to call witnesses to address his apparent mental illness, something he did not want to be part of his defense.

At one point, about a month before trial, Kaczynski apparently agreed to keep his defense lawyers, providing they did not call expert witnesses to address his mental health. When he made his request to represent himself on the eve of trial, the government at first argued to the judge that the trial should go forward with Kaczynski's defense team, but then changed its position and conceded that Kaczynski had a constitutional right to represent himself. Kaczynski eventually pled guilty to the charges.

A defendant can waive his right to an attorney and represent himself before, during, and after trial. At trial, the defendant will commonly have to do more than simply express a desire to represent himself. The court will conduct a hearing to make sure that the defendant understands the charges against him as well as his right to counsel. If the court ascertains that the defendant is intelligently (meaning he understands what he's doing) and voluntarily waiving his right to counsel, the court must allow it. However, the court may decide to appoint a "shadow" counsel anyway, who will be available to consult with the defendant.

A Fool for a Client

We've all heard the maxim: "A lawyer who represents himself has a fool for a client." Well, if a lawyer is a fool to represent himself, how much more so a nonlawyer defendant? Nevertheless, a defendant has an absolute right to represent himself. Whether he can do it well or even competently should have no bearing on the issue. If he has a factual understanding of the charges and the proceedings, he is entitled to his: "Ladies and gentlemen of the jury . . . " moment. He'll just have one fewer person to blame if his next residence is a jail cell.

On occasion a defendant will realize that maybe he should have a lawyer after all. Apparently recognizing that he should have had an attorney to represent him at his latest trial, Dr. Jack Kevorkian hired counsel after being convicted of murder. Kevorkian, known as "Dr. Death," was convicted of second-degree murder and delivery of a controlled substance for his role in the videotaped and televised death of a patient with Lou Gehrig's disease. After the trial, Kevorkian hired for his appeal the lawyer who had helped him gain two acquittals in the past on similar charges.

Ineffective Assistance of Counsel

Not only is a defendant is entitled to counsel, he is entitled to "effective assistance of counsel" under the Sixth Amendment. As a result, if a defendant can make out a claim that she received ineffective assistance of counsel and as a result was convicted (or received a longer sentence than she otherwise would have), her conviction may be overturned.

Logic might dictate a finding of ineffective assistance each time the jury says, "Guilty." The situation sort of speaks for itself, doesn't it? Couldn't a defendant simply argue that his lawyer got an innocent man convicted? He could, but it wouldn't work.

The standard for what constitutes "ineffective assistance" is surprisingly high. The starting point for any review of counsel's performance is the presumption that her assistance was effective. In order to show otherwise, the defendant has to show *specific* errors made by his lawyer. The claim cannot be based on things like the lawyer's general inexperience, lack of preparation time, failure to raise frivolous issues that the defendant wanted raised, failure to object to certain evidence or any decisions that are viewed as "trial tactics." The bottom line: getting a conviction overturned for ineffective assistance of counsel is quite rare.

"The Black Widow of Vegas" episode of *American Justice* (#184) shows just how difficult it can be to make out an ineffective assistance of counsel claim. When the charred remains of wealthy real estate developer Ron Rudin are found, the police investigation focuses on his soft-spoken wife. As the evidence against her mounts (Ron's blood found on a mattress and carpet remnant she discarded, burned remnants of a trunk she used to own found near the body, etc.), she flees. Over a year later she was found by the police (after the story was featured on *America's Most Wanted*) and she went to trial on first-degree murder charges.

Her lawyer gave a rambling, inappropriate opening statement that dealt more with his personal life than the defense of his client. The trial judge even commented that he had never seen or heard anything like that in an opening statement. The defense attorney proceeded to botch the cross-examination of the most important prosecution witness, the defendant's own sister. At one point late in the trial, the defendant actually requested a mistrial based on ineffective assistance of counsel, pointing out her lawyer's many deficiencies to the judge. In fact, her lawyer actually argued to the judge *in support* of the motion, stating that his opening statement had not met the standard of effective assistance. The trial judge denied the motion for mistrial, finding that although not all of the defense counsel's tactics were successful, he at least met the standard of competent counsel.

Finally, a defendant is entitled to *a* lawyer, not a *specific* lawyer. Sure, every defendant in his right mind wanted Johnny Cochran, but no one had a *right* to hear that lyrical cadence in the closing argument at his trial. In fact, the defendant does not even have to like or get along particularly well with his appointed attorney. Unless the attorney-client relationship deteriorates to that point that it makes preparing a defense nearly impossible, the two are stuck like spouses in a bad marriage.

Legal Briefs

Right to counsel—guaranteed by the Fifth and Sixth Amendments; can be waived if waiver is intelligent and voluntary.

Ineffective assistance of counsel—if defendant can show specific errors made by trial counsel (other than strategic decisions, failure to raise frivolous issues, etc.), verdict may be overturned on appeal.

Chapter 30 ⚖️

Guilty Pleas

After one overturned conviction and one mistrial, Dionne Baugh pled guilty to voluntary manslaughter for killing her wealthy lover Lance Herndon. On August 8, 1996, Herndon's nude body was found dead on his waterbed after suffering multiple blows to the head with a blunt object. The police immediately suspected Baugh, although they didn't arrest her until 1998. Baugh was sentenced to ten years in prison and ten more years on probation for voluntary manslaughter.

In her first trial, in 2001, Baugh was convicted of first-degree murder, but that conviction was overturned because the state's case was built entirely on circumstantial evidence and hearsay testimony that the appeals court decided could not support the conviction. In November 2003 the jury in her second trial deadlocked, and a mistrial was declared. Perhaps reluctant to roll the dice a third time, Baugh entered into the plea deal. But why would the prosecution settle for voluntary manslaughter instead of murder?

According to the assistant district attorney on the case, the prosecution "lost an important state witness to cancer who was primarily responsible for gathering a lot of crucial evidence." With a decidedly weaker case, the state apparently decided not to risk an acquittal in a third trial.

In the end, both sides seemed to get what they needed, and another case was disposed of by the criminal justice system.

Guilty pleas are contracts entered into by the defendant and the prosecution. In consideration for the defendant giving up his right to a trial (where she must be proved guilty beyond a reasonable doubt of all elements of the crime—a potentially risky and surely time- and money-burning matter for both sides), the prosecution agrees to reduce the charges or seek a lesser punishment than they might otherwise. A plea deal is much like any other contract a person might enter into, where each side gives some consideration to the other and receives something in return.

Although plea deals seem like straightforward bargains where each side gets something of value, the whole concept is actually quite controversial despite its widespread acceptance. Maybe the sides aren't quite as passionate as with the death penalty, but there are strong arguments both as to why plea bargains are essential and why they are oppressive.

Supporters of the plea bargaining process often focus on its practicality. Plea bargaining is a virtual necessity to keep criminal courts functioning in most states and in the federal system. The *vast majority* of all criminal cases are settled by guilty pleas. If they weren't, you'd be paying a lot more in taxes to support all the new courthouses, judges, bailiffs, court personnel, defense lawyers, assistant district attorneys, etc., that would be necessary to try *five times* as many cases as we do now. Oh, and you could expect to be called for jury duty a whole lot more often, too.

Just as a completely unscientific experiment, spend a few mornings in a criminal courthouse and carefully watch and listen to what goes on just in the corridors, and courtrooms. If your courthouse is anything like most, you'll see and hear a lot of bargaining between defense counsel and prosecutors. Some of this will be casual banter, some more serious whispered actual negotiating, almost all done on a preliminary basis. In some busy city courthouses where dozens of criminal cases are disposed of each day, you may think you're in a bazaar.

Of course, most of the actual deals are made in more formal negotiations in offices or over the phone. But in overcrowded and underfunded criminal systems (the status in most states, particularly in urban areas), lawyers on both sides have to resolve as many cases as possible every day. They do so in as fair and efficient a manner as they can under the circumstances. And that may mean buttonholing the other side in the hallway.

Possibly this strikes you as cavalier, but keep in mind that these same lawyers handle hundreds if not thousands of cases in their careers. Obviously each case is unique and meaningful to the defendant and victims (among others), but the truth is that defense lawyers and prosecutors become fairly adept at analyzing the evidence, the witnesses, the judge, and the strengths and weaknesses of most cases. On top of that, many DA's offices have very specific guidelines for charging offenses and for accepting pleas. It's not quite as random as it might appear, and the truth is, it's the only way to keep the system from completely breaking down.

In addition to the efficiency argument, supporters would say that plea bargains are good because they give defendants a chance to take responsibility. Believe it or not, many people genuinely feel real remorse for their actions; maybe they were out of control because of drugs or alcohol, did something out of character because they were grieving, or had just lost a job or a loved one. Whatever the reason, entering a plea of guilty can be a way of trying to make things right and get some benefit from the prosecutor in the bargain.

Another whole class of people who benefit from plea bargains are the victims and witnesses who are not forced to sit through a trial that could potentially be long and might cause further emotional trauma. While this might not be a relevant consideration in a drug trafficking case, think about rape trials or trials involving young children. A defendant and prosecutor should rightly consider the consequences of a public trial on everyone involved.

On the other hand, there are strong arguments against plea bargaining. Generally speaking, critics would not say that every plea bargain is wrong in and of itself; there are obviously cases where a fair bargain makes sense. What they object to is the wholesale reliance on plea bargaining to make the system work or, in their view, not work.

Some critics suggest that arriving at justice should not resemble negotiating the price of a bicycle at a garage sale; they think it sullies the legal system. Others focus on concerns that are more practical—they think plea bargaining leads to inconsistent results. Some say that plea bargaining lets criminals off too lightly, giving them a "discount" just for saving some judicial resources by avoiding a trial. Still others see plea bargaining as too tough on defendants, putting undue pressure on the innocent to take pleas to lesser charges to escape potentially long sentences if they go to trial.

The Bargain

The requirements for the bargain are that the plea must be "voluntary and intelligent." Again, "voluntary and intelligent" does not necessarily mean "smart." The defendant only has to understand the consequences of her choice (i.e., no trial, no appeal, etc.) and the charge to which she is pleading guilty.

She cannot have been *coerced* into making the bargain. Some would argue that when the prosecutor charges an innocent person (or even overcharges a guilty person) and then offers a significantly reduced charge or lesser sentence that coercion has already taken place. Nevertheless, the criminal justice system relies on the fact that a person, guilty or innocent, can always elect to have a fair trial in front of impartial jurors and that a plea offer is not coercive in and of itself. As long as the defendant understands her options, courts will not find that she has been coerced into pleading guilty.

Even in situations where the prosecution threatens to bring charges that are more serious unless the defendant pleads guilty, courts will not find that the plea deal was made involuntarily. Tough negotiations are par for the course.

Charging Decisions

The police make arrests based on what crime(s) they think the defendant has committed. But once the arrest is made, it is the *prosecutor* who decides what charges the defendant will actually face at trial. Sometimes the prosecutor will agree with the decision of the police, but sometimes he will modify, drop, or add charges. This may happen because of differing views of what charges the evidence will support and sometimes because new evidence is developed after the arrest. In any case, though, the police and prosecutors both routinely bring every charge that is possibly supported by the evidence. The theory is that things will get sorted out at trial (and it's not possible to predict exactly what will happen between the charging decision and the trial, which is probably a year away). Also, both the police and prosecution know that the more charges they bring, the more they have to bargain with in plea negotiations.

The standard procedure for taking a plea is that there will be a hearing where the judge will directly address the defendant. The judge makes certain that the defendant understands:

- the nature of the charge against her
- the maximum penalty for that charge
- that she may plead not guilty, and that by pleading guilty she is giving up her right to a trial.

All of this will be on the record (taken down by a court reporter or recording system). This hearing is usually pretty mechanical, with the judge essentially reading a checklist of questions and the defendant saying the "correct" answers being whispered in her ear by her defense counsel.

In addition, the judge will have to make certain that the defendant is *competent* to enter the plea. The standard for competency in entering a plea is the same as for standing trial; the defendant must have the ability to understand the proceedings going on and to be able to consult in a meaningful way with her attorney.

Curiously, a defendant does *not* have to admit guilt in order to enter a guilty plea. There is no constitutional requirement for an admission of guilt. Pleas of this sort are often called *Alford* pleas, after the Supreme Court case of that name. Where the prosecution has presented strong evidence of guilt, a guilty plea can be an intelligent choice to make. Where the evidence is compelling enough, a defendant can refuse to accept responsibility for the crime while at the same time a judge is accepting his guilty plea. Undoubtedly a judge will scrutinize such pleas stringently to assure that an innocent person is not pleading guilty because of some mental defect of his (or his lawyer), but *Alford* pleas are taken in courts across the country every week.

Enforcing the Bargain

After the court accepts the plea, each side has the right to have the bargain enforced by the court. If the defendant has agreed to cooperate with an investigation or provide testimony in a trial, she must do so or face the original charges. If the prosecution does not keep its end of the deal, the defendant may ask the court to require performance by the prosecution (drop certain charges, etc.) or even ask to withdraw the plea and start negotiations again or have a trial on the original charges.

A defendant is not allowed to get out of her plea deal simply because she regrets having made it. If she sees a codefendants acquitted at trial, she may not withdraw her plea. The basic theory is: "tough luck if you miscalculated your chances at trial." However, if a defendant could show something like ineffective assistance of counsel, where, say, her lawyer completely failed to see that the only evidence against her would likely be suppressed in a pretrial hearing, she may be able to withdraw her plea.

When Kathleen Soliah was captured in 1999 (after years living as homemaker Sara Jane Olson in Minnesota), she faced charges related to an August 1975 attempted bombing of a police car in L.A. She agreed to settle the charges by a plea bargain. On October 31, 2001, she pled guilty to two counts of possessing explosives with intent to murder. All other charges were dropped.

She subsequently announced in the press that she was innocent and was forced to plead guilty because of the country's mood after the September 11, 2001, attacks. This, somewhat predictably, angered the judge who took the plea. Judge Larry Fidler ordered a hearing and asked Olson (she legally changed her name) if she was indeed guilty. She reluctantly said that based on a theory of aiding and abetting that she was guilty.

Then, about a month later, she filed a motion to withdraw her plea because only "cowardice" prevented her from going to trial and that she could not plead guilty when she knew she was not. The judge was not happy. He denied her request and sentenced her to two consecutive ten-years-to-life terms.

Legal Briefs

Guilty plea—a contract between defendant and prosecutor where the defendant agrees to forgo a trial and admit guilt in exchange for the prosecution dropping certain charges or asking for a reduced sentence; must be voluntary and intelligent.

Alford **plea**—where the defendant agrees to plead guilty without actually admitting her guilt.

Chapter 31 ———————————— ⚖

Sentencing

Sentencing doesn't get the attention it deserves. Maybe that's because sentencing lacks the adrenaline rush of an investigation or trial. Once there is a finding (or plea) of guilt, the suspense is broken. But, the action isn't over. Quite a bit can happen at sentencing because this is where society finally gets to settle its score with the defendant. Sentencing may not get the big headlines or the best scenes in *Law & Order: SVU*, but it's still an important topic in criminal law.

Procedural Issues

Following a guilty plea or conviction, the sentence is imposed by the judge. Sentencing is a "critical stage" of a prosecution, and the defendant is entitled to a lawyer at the hearing. Even if the defendant is not given prison time (instead, say, put on probation), he is still entitled to legal representation to make sure that his rights (for example, the right to appeal the sentence) are properly protected (if the intent to appeal must be stated at the hearing, etc.).

Where a defendant's rights *are* curtailed as opposed to other stages of a criminal trial is in the confrontation of witnesses. Unlike at trial where the defendant has the right to confront witnesses, the rule is that the defendant has *no* right to confront witnesses who give information to the judge regarding sentencing. This applies even to capital cases.

Think about that for a moment. You have the right to confront the store owner who has accused you of shoplifting, but (depending on the state) perhaps no right to confront people who may be trying to convince a judge to sentence you to death (presumably for something more serious than shoplifting). The idea is that witnesses at trial serve a different purpose than people who provide information and opinions concerning sentencing.

Of course, the testimony and evidence from the trial will play a major role in sentencing, but the judge can also consider things that were never part of the trial, like the defendant's personal history, the opinions of relevant persons, and even evidence that was excluded from trial because of a Fourth Amendment violation by the police. A judge can also rely on her impression of the defendant's testimony if he takes the stand during trial. The only real restriction on the factors a judge can consider in sentencing is that the information must be reasonably reliable or trustworthy.

PRESENTENCE REPORT

Generally, after a plea or finding of guilt, the judge will request that a "presentence report" be prepared on the defendant and will schedule a hearing in several weeks' time. The presentence report will likely be prepared by the probation department of the court and will cover topics like the defendant's overall criminal history, family and employment history, etc., and any other relevant subjects or subject the judge directs be included. The report will be made available to the judge, the prosecutor, and the defense counsel prior to the sentencing hearing.

The Sentence

In most states the judge is given broad discretion in sentencing, although in some jurisdictions there are sentencing "guidelines" that largely dictate what the sentence should be for each crime. There are also constitutional limits on a judge's discretion. The Eighth Amendment prohibits "cruel and unusual punishment," although if a particular sentence is *allowed* by the state statute, it will usually pass constitutional review (essentially, state legislatures are given deference by the courts). There are circumstances, though, where sentences may be found unconstitutional under the Eighth Amendment.

The first is where the sentence is "grossly disproportionate" to the harm inflicted on society. This comes up frequently where a very lengthy sentence (say twenty years) or even a life sentence is given for a nonviolent offense such as forgery or petty theft. A key factor in these cases is whether there is a possibility of parole; if there is a chance for parole, the lengthy sentence is more likely to be found constitutional.

A sensational example of a harsh sentence that many consider to be disproportionate to the crime involves a seventeen-year-old boy in Georgia who was sentenced to ten years in prison for having consensual oral sex with a fifteen-year-old girl in 2003. Genarlow Wilson was sentenced under an "aggravated child molestation" statute that many criticized specifically because it could lead to a sentence such as this. In 2007 he appealed his sentence on the grounds that it was grossly disproportionate to the crime.

In fact, the legislative sponsor of the aggravated child molestation statute said that the law was intended to "protect kids against really, really bad people doing very bad things" and was "not meant to put kids in jail for oral sex." The Georgia legislature subsequently passed another law that changed the provision that led to Wilson's sentence (the new law would make it only a misdemeanor offense where both parties are minors). Nevertheless, the prosecutor argued that the new law could not be applied retroactively and that the sentence should stand.

In 2007 a judge ordered Wilson released from prison and called the mandatory ten-year sentence "a grave miscarriage of justice." The judge amended Wilson's sentence to misdemeanor aggravated child molestation (which would not only get Wilson out of prison, but would also mean that he would not have to register as a sex offender). Wilson's joy was short-lived, though, as the Georgia attorney general announced he would appeal the judge's order, thereby leaving Wilson in prison at least until the Georgia Supreme Court can resolve the matter.

Another instance where "proportionality" comes up is when the penalty is death and the crime is something other than murder. For example, it is not constitutional to give the death penalty for the crime of raping an adult woman. It is also unconstitutional under the Equal Protection Clause of the Fourteenth Amendment to convert what would be a monetary fine to prison time for those who are unable to afford the fine. It offends our sense of fairness to take the prison option off the table only for those who can afford to pay a fine.

The Death Penalty

Ironically, some normally rational people are so strongly opposed to the idea of state-sanctioned killing that the mere mention of the topic can lead them to want to murder supporters of the death penalty. Without getting into the morality of the death penalty, you can still understand the basic legal principles involved.

ATTITUDES TOWARD THE DEATH PENALTY

A May 2006, Gallup poll (Gallup News Service, June 1, 2006) asked people to choose between the following two approaches to punishing murder: the death penalty or life imprisonment with absolutely no possibility of parole. 47 percent favored the death penalty and 48 percent life imprisonment with no possibility of parole.

Although the death penalty cannot be the *mandatory* punishment for even first-degree murder (the Supreme Court considers that cruel and unusual punishment), the death penalty does *not* constitute cruel and unusual punishment where two basic conditions are met:

- The jury is allowed to consider mitigating and aggravating factors about both the defendant and the crime; and
- There is an appellate review to make sure the death penalty was not imposed based on any discrimination against the defendant.

The "aggravating factors" can be things like the defendant's record of convictions for other crimes of violence or information that he committed the crime for financial gain (although why that should lead to a harsher penalty than a killing committed out of hatred or jealousy is not clear). "Mitigating factors" are broadly construed by courts—anything that would tell a jury about the defendant's character should be allowed, including things like an abusive childhood, mental retardation, or minor participation in the crime.

Until somewhat recently the Supreme Court did not allow "victim impact statements" in death penalty cases because they wanted to avoid the possibility that the defendant would be sentenced to death based purely on sympathy. However, the Court now allows the victim's family to weigh in and perhaps balance the mitigating information presented by the defendant.

There are other limitations on imposing the death penalty. As noted above, the Supreme Court has held that it is unconstitutional to give the death penalty for rape of an adult woman (the penalty is disproportionate to the crime). It is also unconstitutional to give the death penalty to a defendant who is presently insane (even if she was sane when the crime was committed and competent to stand trial). There is also a question of whether it is permissible to give the death penalty to defendants who are younger than sixteen. See, even Supreme Court Justices have hearts.

Legal Briefs

Presentence report—a report usually prepared by the probation department providing information about the defendant relative to her sentencing (education, employment history, criminal history).

Cruel and unusual punishment—usually found where the sentence is "grossly disproportionate" to the harm inflicted on society.

Death penalty—cannot be a mandatory sentence; allowed where two conditions are met:

- jury is allowed to consider mitigating and aggravating factors about the defendant and the crime, and;
- there is an appellate review to make sure the penalty was not based on discrimination.

Chapter 32 ——————————— ⚖�

Double Jeopardy

"The Fifth Amendment's provision that no person can be twice put in jeopardy for the same offense."

"What is 'double jeopardy,' Alex?"

"Correct. You are our new leader with thirty-eight hundred dollars. Back after this commercial break."

As both Alex Trebek and the contestants undoubtedly know, double jeopardy applies not only to federal prosecutions, but is a fundamental right that the Supreme Court has said applies to the states via the Due Process Clause of the Fourteenth Amendment.

Double jeopardy is a simple proposition: a person who commits an offense can only be subjected to one prosecution for that offense. If there is either a conviction or an acquittal, the criminal matter is complete. This means that a defendant won't have to live the rest of her life in fear of subsequent prosecution and also that the government doesn't get the benefit of going to trial a second or even third time after learning all about the defense case.

When "Jeopardy" Begins

A crucial question in analyzing double jeopardy issues when the defendant is actually "in jeopardy," so that society knows that he can't be put there again. Fancy-pants lawyers refer to this as when jeopardy "attaches." There is actually a specific moment in a criminal proceeding when this happens.

In a jury trial, jeopardy attaches when the jury is empaneled and sworn in; in a nonjury trial, when the first witness is sworn in. Generally, once jeopardy attaches, the defendant gets his trial and society lives with the results. This being the law, however, there are exceptions.

CIVIL TRIALS

Double jeopardy only applies to criminal trials; the state can bring a civil action based on the same event even when the defendant has already faced (or is about to face) a criminal trial. Similarly, a citizen may sue a defendant who has already been tried, even if the defendant was acquitted in the criminal matter—which is what Ron Goldman's parents famously did in suing OJ Simpson after he was acquitted in the "trial of the century."

Mistrials

If a mistrial is declared by the judge because the defendant asked for one (or consents to a mistrial), the jeopardy bar is waived. When the defendant asks for the mistrial, he has waived his double jeopardy protection and the government may (but is not required to) retry the case. Double jeopardy does not mean that there can never be two trials, only that there can't be a retrial after a decision has actually been reached on the merits of the criminal case.

There are also instances where a mistrial can be declared *without* the defendant's consent. If the defendant objects to the mistrial (for example, he thinks things are going his way in the trial), the judge can only declare a mistrial where there is a "manifest necessity" to do so. Basically, "manifest necessity" means that in the judge's view the interests of society would not be served by a continuation of this particular trial.

Manifest necessity is most often found where the jury is unable to reach a verdict (a "hung jury"). In 2001, Cherry Hills, New Jersey, Rabbi Fred Neulander was tried for arranging the murder of his wife, Carol Neulander, who was found beaten to death in their home in 1994. The case made national headlines because of the sordid details, including Fred Neulander's affair with a radio personality who threatened to leave him if he didn't become a single man. Perhaps his religious convictions precluded divorce, so instead he had his wife murdered.

The trial lasted almost three months, and after seven days of deliberations the jury failed to reach a verdict. This is the kind of thing that is meant by the term "manifest necessity"; the jury presumably worked diligently but just couldn't come to agreement. The judge decided that further deliberations wouldn't be useful and declared a mistrial. The prosecutor almost immediately decided that he would again pursue the case, and Neulander was retried and convicted. In 2003 he was sentenced to life in prison.

There are other situations where manifest necessity can be found. If the defendant or her counsel causes a mistrial by making it impossible to have a fair trial (saying prejudicial or improper things in front of the jury), the judge can declare a mistrial and double jeopardy would not prevent a retrial.

Appeals

If the defendant successfully appeals his conviction, he has waived his right to the protection of the double jeopardy clause. If Fred Neulander's successfully appealed his conviction, the state would undoubtedly try him again and Neulander wouldn't have a legal basis to object to this new trial.

The general rule is that the retrial cannot be for a greater offense than at the first trial. In other words, if the defendant is convicted of manslaughter and the conviction is overturned, he cannot be retried for murder. Likewise, the defendant cannot be retried for a greater *degree* of offense (no retrying for first-degree murder where the original conviction was for second-degree murder).

Interestingly, when a defendant is convicted for the same offense after a successful appeal on his first conviction, double jeopardy does *not* prohibit a greater punishment than was given for the first conviction (although the judge may have to show new facts warranting the harsher sentence in order to avoid other constitutional problems). As usual, there is an exception to this rule that applies to the death penalty. In jurisdictions where the death penalty can only be imposed through a separate process after conviction and it is *not* imposed, the defendant cannot face the death penalty in a retrial after appeal.

The prosecution may not appeal an acquittal after trial; that's precisely what the double jeopardy clause prohibits. However, the prosecution may appeal orders made by the trial judge if the orders are made before jeopardy attaches (say, where the judge dismisses an indictment at a pretrial hearing). The prosecution may also appeal in instances where the judge sets aside a guilty verdict because a reversal of that order will not require a second trial for the defendant.

Same Offense

Double jeopardy applies only when the defendant is being tried for the *same offense* in a second trial. According to the Blockburger test, after the case of that name, two crimes are considered the same offense unless each requires proof of an additional element that the other crime does not require. Determining whether two crimes are the same offense essentially just requires a mechanical analysis of the specific elements of each crime.

Some general rules apply. Conspiracy and the actual offense are separate crimes (remember, the "conspiracy" is the agreement itself). A single act can involve separate crimes (breaking into a rival's apartment to assault him might seem like one event, but it can clearly involve separate crimes of burglary and assault).

Legal Briefs

Double jeopardy—prohibits a defendant from being tried twice for the same offense.

When jeopardy attaches—when the jury is sworn in; in a nonjury trial, when the first witness is sworn in.

Mistrials—if the defendant requests a mistrial, double jeopardy is waived; double jeopardy does not apply where a mistrial is declared because of "manifest necessity" (usually a hung jury).

Appeals—where the defendant appeals and his conviction is overturned, double jeopardy is waived; second trial generally cannot be for a greater offense than the first trial, although there can be a greater punishment.

Same offense—two crimes are considered the same offense *unless* each requires proof of an additional element that the other does not.

Index

About the Author

JIM SILVER is a former Assistant United States Attorney who prosecuted criminal cases in Washington, D.C., and argued before the United States Court of Appeals for the District of Columbia Circuit. Prior to that he was a civil litigator at one of the nation's largest law firms. For the past ten years he has been an at-home dad and writer.